Apress Pocket Guides

Apress Pocket Guides present concise summaries of cutting-edge developments and working practices throughout the tech industry. Shorter in length, books in this series aims to deliver quick-to-read guides that are easy to absorb, perfect for the time-poor professional.

This series covers the full spectrum of topics relevant to the modern industry, from security, AI, machine learning, cloud computing, web development, product design, to programming techniques and business topics too.

Typical topics might include:

- A concise guide to a particular topic, method, function or framework
- Professional best practices and industry trends
- A snapshot of a hot or emerging topic
- Industry case studies
- Concise presentations of core concepts suited for students and those interested in entering the tech industry
- Short reference guides outlining 'need-to-know' concepts and practices.

More information about this series at `https://link.springer.com/bookseries/17385`.

Practical Angular Signals

Levelling Up Your Web Development Skills with Signals, Patterns and Architectures

Sonu Kapoor

Foreword by Mark Thompson,
Sr. Developer Relations Engineer, Google

Apress®

Practical Angular Signals: Levelling Up Your Web Development Skills with Signals, Patterns and Architectures

Sonu Kapoor
Brampton, ON, Canada

ISBN-13 (pbk): 979-8-8688-2006-9   ISBN-13 (electronic): 979-8-8688-2007-6
https://doi.org/10.1007/979-8-8688-2007-6

Copyright © 2025 by Sonu Kapoor

This work is subject to copyright. All rights are reserved by the Publisher, whether the whole or part of the material is concerned, specifically the rights of translation, reprinting, reuse of illustrations, recitation, broadcasting, reproduction on microfilms or in any other physical way, and transmission or information storage and retrieval, electronic adaptation, computer software, or by similar or dissimilar methodology now known or hereafter developed.

Trademarked names, logos, and images may appear in this book. Rather than use a trademark symbol with every occurrence of a trademarked name, logo, or image we use the names, logos, and images only in an editorial fashion and to the benefit of the trademark owner, with no intention of infringement of the trademark.

The use in this publication of trade names, trademarks, service marks, and similar terms, even if they are not identified as such, is not to be taken as an expression of opinion as to whether or not they are subject to proprietary rights.

While the advice and information in this book are believed to be true and accurate at the date of publication, neither the authors nor the editors nor the publisher can accept any legal responsibility for any errors or omissions that may be made. The publisher makes no warranty, express or implied, with respect to the material contained herein.

> Managing Director, Apress Media LLC: Welmoed Spahr
> Acquisitions Editor: Anandadeep Roy
> Editorial Assistant: Jessica Vakili

Cover designed by eStudioCalamar

Distributed to the book trade worldwide by Springer Science+Business Media New York, 1 New York Plaza, New York, NY 10004. Phone 1-800-SPRINGER, fax (201) 348-4505, e-mail orders-ny@springer-sbm.com, or visit www.springeronline.com. Apress Media, LLC is a Delaware LLC and the sole member (owner) is Springer Science + Business Media Finance Inc (SSBM Finance Inc). SSBM Finance Inc is a **Delaware** corporation.

For information on translations, please e-mail booktranslations@springernature.com; for reprint, paperback, or audio rights, please e-mail bookpermissions@springernature.com.

Apress titles may be purchased in bulk for academic, corporate, or promotional use. eBook versions and licenses are also available for most titles. For more information, reference our Print and eBook Bulk Sales web page at http://www.apress.com/bulk-sales.

Any source code or other supplementary material referenced by the author in this book is available to readers on GitHub. For more detailed information, please visit https://www.apress.com/gp/services/source-code.

If disposing of this product, please recycle the paper

Table of Contents

About the Author ix

About the Technical Reviewer xi

Introduction xiii

Foreword xv

Chapter 1: Setting Up the Signals-First Shopping Cart App 1

Project Goals 1

    Starting a Standalone Angular App 2

Summary 11

Chapter 2: Modeling Product and Cart State with Signals 13

Folder Structure Update 14

Defining the Cart Item Model 14

    Why Store Full Product Objects Instead of Just IDs? 15

    Creating the Cart Service 15

    Sidebar: What About NgRx Selectors? 19

    Integrating the Cart 20

    Architectural Note 23

Summary 24

Chapter 3: Effects, APIs, and Async Data with Signals 25

Folder Structure Update 26

    Refactoring ProductService with httpResource() 26

    What httpResource() Gives You 28

v

TABLE OF CONTENTS

Triggering Fetches Reactively 30
Understanding effect(): Reactive Side Effects Made Simple 31
    Important Note on effect() and Injection Context 32
    Displaying Data with httpResource() 34
    Working with External APIs 40
    NgRx Effects vs. Signal Effects 40
    Architectural Note 41
What You Should See in the Browser 42
Summary 43

Chapter 4: Component Communication with Signals 45

Folder Structure Update 46
Creating a Shared Cart Header Component 46
    Rendering the Header in the Shell 49
    Passing Signals to Child Components 50
    Architectural Note 52
    Comparison Note: Without Signals 53
    Summary 54

Chapter 5: Routing, Guards, and Auth with Signals 57

Folder Structure Update 58
Creating the Authentication Service 58
Creating a Login Page 60
Creating a Checkout Page and Route Guard 62
    Create the Guard 63
    Protecting the Route 64
    A Minimal Checkout View 65
    Try It Yourself 65
    Controlling Access to Cart Actions 66

TABLE OF CONTENTS

Updating the Header to Show Auth State 68
Architectural Note 73
    Why This Is Cleaner Than NgRx 73
    What About Signal Routers? 74
    Why This Matters in the Real World 74
Summary 75

Chapter 6: Testing, Debugging, and Performance Tuning 77

Why We Skipped Tests Until Now 77
Folder Structure Update 78
Writing Tests for Signal-Based Services 78
    Comparing Signal-Based Tests to RxJS-Based Tests 82
Testing Signal-Driven Components 83
    Test Setup 85
    Test: Should Show a Login Button 87
    Test: Should Display Total Items from the Cart Service Signal 87
Debugging Signals with Angular DevTools 89
Debugging with Inline Effects 90
Signal Hygiene: Patterns That Scale 91
Summary 92

Chapter 7: From RxJS to Signals – Migration and Interoperability 95

Working Alongside RxJS 96
Introducing linkedSignal() – Controlled Bridging with External State 96
Architectural Decision: Push vs. Pull 98
NgRx Store Migration – A Deep Dive 99
    Replacing Selectors with Computed Signals 99
    Replacing Reducers with Signal State 100
    Replacing Effects with effect() and Async Data with linkedSignal() 101

vii

TABLE OF CONTENTS

Replacing Store Dispatches with Method Calls 104
A Realistic Migration Path 104
When NgRx Still Makes Sense 104
Summary 105

Chapter 8: Completing the Cart Experience with a Sidebar 107
Chapter Goals 107
Folder Structure Update 108
    UI Service 109
    Building the Cart Component 110
    Sidebar Styling 112
    Building the Cart Sidebar Component 114
    Sidebar Template 115
    Sidebar Styling 116
    Header Enhancements 119
    Checkout Page 121
    UI Integration in App Component 123
    Summary 125

Chapter 9: Final Words – Signals in Action 127
A Fully Reactive Shopping Cart 127
Simpler, Smaller, and Stronger 129
What We Left Out 129
Where to Go from Here 130

About the Author

Sonu Kapoor is a Google Developer Expert in Angular and a Microsoft Most Valuable Professional (MVP), first awarded in 2005 and again in 2024, with over two decades of experience in software engineering. He has led engineering initiatives at top-tier global companies, including Cisco, Citigroup, and Sony. At Citigroup, he architected the frontend for their global trading system, while at Sony, he played a key role in large-scale migration projects that modernized legacy platforms using Angular.

Sonu is a trusted contributor to the Angular framework, having co-authored the Typed Forms RFC – the most upvoted feature request in Angular's history. He is a member of the exclusive Angular Collaborators group, working alongside the core team at Google to influence the future of the framework.

He has authored and co-authored several books, including *AI-Powered App Development* and *Beginning JavaScript Syntax*. Sonu is also a technical editor, research paper reviewer, and frequent international speaker. Earlier in his career, he founded DotNetSlackers.com, a developer portal that served over 33 million views and helped shape the early .NET ecosystem.

About the Technical Reviewer

Rainer Hahnekamp is a Google Developer Expert (GDE) and a trusted collaborator on the NgRx team, where he actively contributes to its maintenance and extension. In addition to NgRx, Rainer also maintains and actively extends other significant open source libraries. These include ngrx-toolkit, a set of powerful extensions specifically designed for the NgRx SignalStore, and Sheriff, a valuable tool that introduces clear modules, boundaries, and dependency rules to any TypeScript project, enhancing code organization and maintainability. Furthermore, Rainer is currently working on Testronaut, an innovative library focused on providing robust component testing capabilities through Playwright. He is also a dedicated trainer and consultant within the Angular Architects expert network and runs ng-news, a popular weekly Angular newsletter.

Introduction

The Angular landscape is undergoing a significant transformation with the introduction of Signals. Traditionally, Angular has relied heavily on RxJS and `@Input()`/`@Output()` bindings to manage data flow and change detection. While this approach has served Angular developers well, it comes with a set of challenges: boilerplate-heavy code, unpredictable reactivity, and a steep learning curve for newcomers.

Signals mark a paradigm shift. They offer a more intuitive, fine-grained, and performant way to express state and reactivity in Angular applications. With Signals, Angular moves closer to the reactive primitives seen in frameworks like SolidJS, while preserving its unique advantages like dependency injection and powerful tooling.

This book is a deep dive into Angular Signals from a service-based state management perspective. Rather than relying on plain objects or patterns unfamiliar to enterprise developers, we advocate for structuring your state logic using Angular services, an approach that naturally fits with existing Angular paradigms and scales effectively.

You'll learn how to build maintainable, testable, and high-performance applications using Signals. We'll walk through real-world examples, show how to replace common RxJS patterns, and guide you in designing reactive services that integrate cleanly with the Angular ecosystem. Whether you're upgrading an existing Angular app or starting from scratch, this book will equip you with the tools and mindset to leverage Signals for better code clarity, maintainability, and performance.

Foreword

Angular took a bold step in reinventing itself with the addition of Signals to the API surface. The intentions were not to bloat the API with tools that don't serve developers but instead to provide developers with the critical infrastructure required to build scalable web applications that serve their users. We wanted to place developers in a winning position – one where they could create applications their users will love. We've done that with the introduction of Signals to the Angular community. As we continue to mature and expand the API surface, developers will need real-world insights that empower them to build great applications. Sonu's book does just that.

Anyone can go to the documentation for a new API and learn the fundamentals, but often that isn't enough. Developers need to go beyond the basics into real-world, tested patterns and structure. This book is a great resource for any developer looking to do just that. This book doesn't try to cover the entire scope of Angular but, instead, sharply focuses on Signals – much to the developer's benefit. Readers are treated to concise, informative patterns from a professional developer who has built scalable production solutions. I'm excited for those fortunate enough to use this book as a companion to their Angular Signals learning journey because I'm certain that through Sonu's expert guidance, they will transform their applications, teams, and career.

—Mark Thompson, Sr. Developer Relations Engineer, Google

CHAPTER 1

Setting Up the Signals-First Shopping Cart App

To build a Signals-first Angular application, we need more than a few `signal()` calls sprinkled across components. We need to rethink how we structure, encapsulate, and propagate state. This chapter lays the foundation for a shopping cart application that will evolve throughout the book, and every decision here, from folder layout to state management, will shape the reactivity model used in the rest of the project.

We'll scaffold a standalone Angular app, organize it for scalability, define a signal-powered service for managing product data, and wire up our first visual component to verify reactive updates.

Project Goals

We're building a shopping cart, not as a toy example, but because it reflects the kinds of reactive patterns developers face in real-world applications. From dynamic UI updates and derived totals to loading async data and guarding navigation flows, this app will touch on

CHAPTER 1   SETTING UP THE SIGNALS-FIRST SHOPPING CART APP

- Real-time reactivity with signals
- Derived state using computed()
- Async state via httpResource
- Signal-based route guards and conditions
- Testable, modular services with minimal boilerplate

By the end of the book, you'll have a full-featured, reactive Angular application powered entirely by signals and services, without relying on RxJS or global state libraries. Figure 1-1 shows how the cart will look at the end of the book.

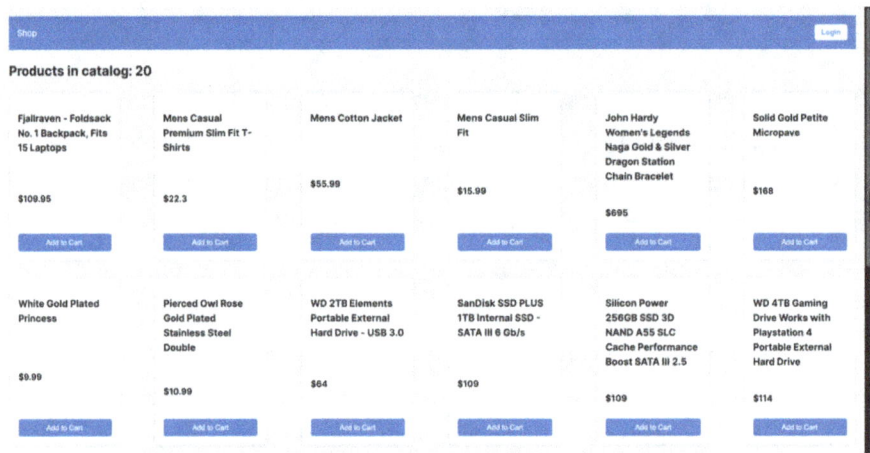

Figure 1-1. *Shopping Cart*

Starting a Standalone Angular App

To generate a clean, standalone project without generating any unit tests and using the Angular CLI, run the below command (Listing 1-1).

CHAPTER 1   SETTING UP THE SIGNALS-FIRST SHOPPING CART APP

Listing 1-1. Generating the Project

```
npx @angular/cli@latest new signals-cart --standalone --routing
--style=scss
cd signals-cart
```

Make sure to enable

- Standalone components
- Routing
- SCSS styling

Once scaffolded, open the project in VS Code.

Project Structure

We'll begin organizing our app for scale by introducing folders for models, services, and route-level components. Table 1-1 shows the intended structure.

Table 1-1. *Initial Folder Structure of src/app*

Folder	Purpose
models/	Shared interfaces like Product
services/	Signal-powered state containers
pages/	Route-level components like Home
pages/home/	Home components files (.ts, .html, .scss)
app.routes.ts	Root route configuration
app.config.ts	Bootstrap configuration for the standalone app

This structure gives us a foundation we'll build on incrementally across chapters.

New Extensions

Starting in Angular 20, the CLI removes the default file extensions. In this book, we will keep using the pre-20 extensions. Update your angular.json and include the following schematics from Listing 1-2.

Listing 1-2. Angular.json Changes to Maintain Previous Angular Extensions

```
"schematics": {
  "@schematics/angular:component": {
    "style": "scss",
    "type": "component"
  },
  "@schematics/angular:directive": { "type": "directive" },
  "@schematics/angular:service": { "type": "service" },
  "@schematics/angular:guard": { "typeSeparator": "." },
  "@schematics/angular:interceptor": { "typeSeparator": "."   },
  "@schematics/angular:module": { "typeSeparator": "." },
  "@schematics/angular:pipe": { "typeSeparator": "." }
},
```

Creating the Product Model

Since we are building a shopping cart, we will need a list of products. Let's start to create src/app/models/product.model.ts and define a simple Product interface (Listing 1-3).

Listing 1-3. Product Interface

```
// src/app/models/product.model.ts

export interface Product {
  id: string;
  title: string;
  price: number;
}
```

We'll enrich this model in later chapters with things like ratings or categories, but for now, this is enough to simulate a catalog.

Modeling Product State with Signals in a Service

Now let's build our first state container, a service powered by Angular Signals. This service will manage our list of products and create a simple loading state. Generate the product service using the below command.

```
npx ng generate service services/product --skip-tests
```

Define the following service (Listing 1-4).

Listing 1-4. Product Service

```
// src/app/services/product.service.ts

import { Injectable, signal, computed } from '@angular/core';
import { Product } from '../models/product.model';

@Injectable({ providedIn: 'root' })
export class ProductService {
  #products = signal<Product[]>([]);
  #loading = signal(false);
```

CHAPTER 1 SETTING UP THE SIGNALS-FIRST SHOPPING CART APP

```
  readonly products = this.#products.asReadonly();
  readonly loading = this.#loading.asReadonly();
  readonly count = computed(() => this.#products().length);

  constructor() {
    this.#loading.set(true);
    setTimeout(() => {
      this.#products.set([
        {
          id: 'p1',
          title: 'Demo Product',
          price: 99,
        }
      ]);
      this.#loading.set(false);
    }, 1000);
  }

  setLoading(isLoading: boolean) {
    this.#loading.set(isLoading);
  }
}
```

In this service, we are using a `signal()` to create reactive state variables. These are like `BehaviorSubject`s but with automatic dependency tracking and without the RxJS overhead.

- `#products` is our internal signal holding the array of products.
- `#loading` is a boolean flag to show the loading state.
- `asReadonly()` exposes the signal to the outside world but prevents external mutation.
- `count` is a derived signal that calculates the total number of products using `computed()`.

Note for advanced readers The loading signal and setTimeout shown here is a temporary pattern. In Chapter 3, we'll switch to Angular's httpResource, which provides its own built-in loading, error, and data signals. At that point, the manual setLoading() method and #loading signal will be removed. For now, this simplified version helps us focus on core signal concepts without layering in async complexity too early.

Displaying Product Count in the Home Page

Let's generate a standalone (pages/home) component to render the product count. Make sure to first create the pages folder and change the directory into that.

```
npx ng generate component pages/home --standalone --skip-tests
```

Update the component class as seen in Listing 1-5.

Listing 1-5. Home Component Class

```
// src/app/pages/home/home.component.ts

import { Component } from '@angular/core';
import { CommonModule } from '@angular/common';
import { ProductService } from '../../services/product.service';

@Component({
  selector: 'app-home',
  standalone: true,
  imports: [CommonModule],
  templateUrl: './home.component.html',
```

CHAPTER 1 SETTING UP THE SIGNALS-FIRST SHOPPING CART APP

```
  changeDetection: ChangeDetectionStrategy.OnPush,
})
export class HomeComponent {
  private readonly productService = inject(ProductService);

  count = this.productService.count;
  loading = this.productService.loading;
}
```

We've also added `changeDetection: ChangeDetectionStrategy.OnPush` to our component. This tells Angular to optimize change detection by skipping parts of the component tree unless an input changes.

In previous Angular versions, using `OnPush` came with tradeoffs: Angular wouldn't detect changes unless they came through `@Input()` bindings or you manually triggered them via `ChangeDetectorRef.markForCheck()`. This often made state management more complex.

But with Signals, Angular is now aware of exactly what reactive values your view depends on. When those values change, Angular knows to update the DOM - even with `OnPush` enabled. This means you get the same performance benefits, without needing to worry about manual detection or when to call `markForCheck()`. In essence, Signals make `OnPush` frictionless.

Since all the state in this app will be powered by signals, we can safely use `OnPush` across the board, with zero boilerplate.

And update the template (Listing 1-6) using Angular's control flow syntax and using the exposed Signals from the product service.

Listing 1-6. Home Component Template

```
<!-- src/app/pages/home/home.component.html -->
@if (loading()) {
  <p>Loading products...</p>
```

```
} @else {
  <h2>Products in catalog: {{ count() }}</h2>
}
```

In this template, we are using the `loading` and `count` Signals. But why are those functions?

Fine-Grained Change Detection in the Template

When you call a signal like `loading()` or `count()` (Listing 1-5) inside the template, Angular tracks it precisely and only updates the affected DOM when its value changes.

Angular knows that this block depends on the `loading` Signal. So, when the signal is updated, e.g., from `true` to `false` after the data loads, Angular updates just this part of the DOM, not the entire component. So, when Angular **automatically tracks this usage**, it knows

- Which signal values were read during rendering
- Which parts of the DOM depend on those values
- When to update only the affected DOM nodes (and nothing else!)

Important This is called fine-grained change detection. It's a major performance win and removes the need for tools like `ChangeDetectorRef` or `OnPush`.

Every signal used in a template is automatically tracked in this way, whether in `@if`, `@for`, or simple interpolations. Angular updates only what's needed, when it's needed.

Routing to the Home Page

Before we can see anything in the browser, let's add some simple routing (Listing 1-7). Create the file src/app/app.routes.ts and define the root route, as shown in Listing 1-7.

Listing 1-7. Routing

```
import { Routes } from '@angular/router';
import { HomeComponent } from './pages/home/home.component';

export const routes: Routes = [
  {
    path: '',
    component: HomeComponent
  }
];
```

Replace the contents of app.component.html with just the outlet:

```
<router-outlet />
```

Now run the application using the below command:

```
npx ng serve
```

You should see "Loading products..." for a second, followed by Products in catalog 1 (Figure 1-2).

Products in catalog: 1

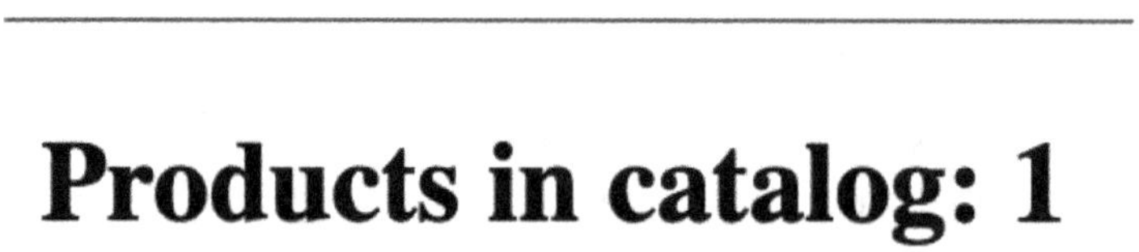

Figure 1-2. *Products*

This confirms our signals are reactive and updates the view as expected.

Architectural Note

By using Angular services as reactive state containers, we avoid component bloat and enable shared state across multiple parts of the app.

For example, the product service can later be used by the cart page, the checkout view, and even a future admin panel - all without duplicating logic.

This approach is more modular, to test, and fits naturally with Angular's dependency injection system. This approach has several benefits:

- It keeps state local to the feature or module.
- It enables easy mocking during tests.
- It allows access to other Angular dependencies (like Router, ActivatedRoute, etc.) without compromise.
- It avoids the pitfalls of global state trees or complex store libraries.

By organizing our application around a service-based state, we align with Angular's design philosophy while gaining the clarity and control that Signals offer.

Summary

In this chapter, we scaffolded a standalone Angular project and introduced a signal-first architecture powered by Angular services. We created a minimal `ProductService`, used `signal()` and `computed()` to manage reactivity, and displayed derived state in a standalone `HomeComponent`.

CHAPTER 1   SETTING UP THE SIGNALS-FIRST SHOPPING CART APP

We also saw the first use of Angular's new control flow syntax, which eliminates the need for structural directives like *ngIf. More importantly, we demonstrated how signals can be read directly in the template, enabling Angular's fine-grained change detection. The DOM updates automatically when signals change, without requiring manual subscriptions, change detection logic, or teardown steps.

To take full advantage of this, we configured our component with `ChangeDetectionStrategy.OnPush`. Thanks to the dependency tracking built into signals, Angular can now update the view efficiently and precisely, with no additional work from us.

From this point forward, the application will grow feature by feature, chapter by chapter, always with a clear reactivity model and consistent architectural structure. In the next chapter, we'll introduce a signal-powered cart service and implement reactive totals and line item logic.

CHAPTER 2

Modeling Product and Cart State with Signals

In the previous chapter, we created an Angular application and built our first signal-powered service to manage the product catalog. That was just the beginning. In this chapter, we introduce the shopping cart, define a model for cart items, and implement a dedicated service to manage it. We'll also begin deriving useful reactive state using `computed()`, things like item count and total cost.

Rather than adding a full cart view, we'll keep our changes limited to the `HomeComponent`. This lets us gradually evolve the app without overwhelming the structure or the reader.

Folder Structure Update

We are adding one model and one service in this chapter.

Table 2-1. *Continued Folder Structure of src/app*

Folder	Purpose
models/	Adds cart-item.model.ts to represent cart state
services/	Adds cart.service.ts to encapsulate cart logic

This structure will remain stable for a few chapters, until we begin separating pages like cart, checkout, and product details.

Defining the Cart Item Model

Let's begin by defining a new `CartItem` model. This model pairs a product with a quantity and allows us to compute things like totals and line items.

```
// src/app/models/cart-item.model.ts

import { Product } from './product.model';

export interface CartItem {
  product: Product;
  quantity: number;
}
```

Why Store Full Product Objects Instead of Just IDs?

Although storing product IDs is common in state management for normalization, in this context, it makes more sense to store full product references directly in the cart. This approach simplifies rendering and calculating totals since we avoid extra lookups or joins. It's a pragmatic choice that prioritizes simplicity over strict normalization.

Creating the Cart Service

Our cart logic lives entirely inside a new service. This service encapsulates the cart's internal state using signals and exposes computed values for the item count and total price. This service (Listing 2-1) will hold the internal state of the cart using signals and expose derived signals for

- List of items
- Total item count
- Total price
- Empty check

Listing 2-1. Generating the Cart Service

```
// src/app/services/cart.service.ts

import { computed, Injectable, signal } from '@angular/core';
import { CartItem } from '../models/cart-item.model';
import { Product } from '../models/product.model';

@Injectable({ providedIn: 'root' })
export class CartService {
  #items = signal<CartItem[]>([]);
```

CHAPTER 2   MODELING PRODUCT AND CART STATE WITH SIGNALS

```
  readonly items = this.#items.asReadonly();

  readonly totalItems = computed(() =>
    this.#items().reduce((sum, item) =>
      sum + item.quantity, 0)
  );

  readonly totalPrice = computed(() =>
    this.#items().reduce((sum, item) =>
      sum + item.quantity * item.product.price, 0)
);

  readonly isEmpty = computed(() =>
    this.#items().length === 0);

  constructor() {
    // Automatically persist cart to
    // localStorage on any cart change
    effect(() => {
      localStorage.setItem('cart',
        JSON.stringify(this._items()));
    });
  }

  addProduct(product: Product) {
    const current = this.#items();
    const index = current.findIndex((i) =>
      i.product.id === product.id);

    if (index >= 0) {
      const updated = [...current];
      updated[index] = {
        ...updated[index],
        quantity: updated[index].quantity + 1,
      };
```

```
      this.#items.set(updated);
    } else {
      this.#items.set([...current,
        { product, quantity: 1 }]);
      }
    }
  }

  removeProduct(productId: string) {
    this.#items.set(this.#items().filter((i) =>
      i.product.id !== productId));
  }

  clear() {
    this.#items.set([]);
  }
}
```

This single service gives us a fully reactive cart: the list of items, the total quantity, and the total price.

Let's take a closer look at how this works.

Each of the derived values, totalItems, totalPrice, and isEmpty, is created using the computed() function. These are derived signals, meaning Angular tracks their dependencies automatically. We've also added an effect() to persist the cart state into localStorage. This kind of side effect is common in real-world apps and is now easy to express declaratively with Angular Signals. Any time the cart updates, this effect will run automatically and persist the updated state – no lifecycle hooks or subscriptions required.

- signal<CartItem[]>([]) creates reactive state for the cart items.

- asReadonly() ensures components can read from but not mutate the state.

- computed() is used for derived state: total quantity, price, and empty check.

- addProduct() updates the quantity if a product already exists in the cart or adds a new entry.

- removeProduct() removes the specific product from the cart.

- clear() removes all items from the cart.

For example, take a look at the example in Listing 2-2.

Listing 2-2. Computing the Total Items

```
readonly totalItems = computed(() =>
  this.#items().reduce((sum, item) => sum + item.quantity, 0)
);
```

This signal depends on the current value of #items. Whenever the internal #items signal changes, such as when a product is added or removed, Angular will re-evaluate totalItems() and update the UI wherever it's used.

Note There are no manual subscriptions. There's no need to trigger change detection. Angular tracks all dependencies automatically, down to the expression level.

This is what makes signals so powerful: your application becomes automatically reactive, with zero boilerplate.

CHAPTER 2 MODELING PRODUCT AND CART STATE WITH SIGNALS

Sidebar: What About NgRx Selectors?

If you've used NgRx in the past, you might be familiar with this kind of derived state using selectors. For example, Listing 2-3 shows how the total item count might be modeled in a typical NgRx store.

Listing 2-3. RxJS Comparison to Retrieve the Total Items

```
export const selectCartItems =
createFeatureSelector<CartItem[]>('cart');

export const selectTotalItems = createSelector(
  selectCartItems,
  (items) => items.reduce((sum, item) =>
    sum + item.quantity, 0)
);
```

You would then inject `Store` into your component and call `.select(selectTotalItems)`, often with an `async` pipe, and maybe wrap it in a `ChangeDetectionStrategy.OnPush` component. It works, but it requires a lot of indirection, naming decisions, and again repeated boilerplate code.

- You define state in reducers
- Then extract it via feature selectors
- Then compose it via memoized selectors
- Then subscribe in your component
- And then test all that in isolation

With Signals, it's just as shown in Listing 2-4.

Listing 2-4. Computing the Total Items Using Signals

```
readonly totalItems = computed(() =>
  this.#items().reduce((sum, item) =>
    sum + item.quantity, 0)
);
```

There's no need to register selectors, no memoization worries, and no need to orchestrate state via dispatch + reducers. The signal is scoped to the service, and Angular tracks it wherever it's used in the UI. With Signals, the mental model around reactivity becomes so much simpler.

> **Note** The derived state becomes intuitive and local, and still testable.

This is what makes Signals such a powerful tool: you keep the benefits of a reactive architecture without the indirection.

Integrating the Cart

We'll now wire the cart service into our existing HomeComponent. This lets us track how many items have been added and display them on the home page. We'll also allow users to add products to the cart directly from this view. In a future chapter, we will move some of this logic into a product list component.

First, we inject the CartService and expose the derived totalItems signal using a local alias cartCount.

We now also expose the list of products from ProductService. Both products and cartCount are signals, which means the DOM will update automatically when they change. Listing 2-5 shows the implementation. To keep the code simple, we have removed the previous imported classes; however, the supplied code with this book will have the complete set of imports.

CHAPTER 2   MODELING PRODUCT AND CART STATE WITH SIGNALS

This approach keeps the component declarative.

Listing 2-5. Updating the Home Component Class

```
// src/app/pages/home/home.component.ts

...
import { CartService } from '../../services/cart.service';
import { Product } from '../../models/product.model';

export class HomeComponent {
  private readonly productService = inject(ProductService);
  private readonly cartService = inject(CartService);

  products = this.productService.products;
  loading = this.productService.loading;
  cartCount = this.cartService.totalItems;
  addToCart(productId: string) {
    const product = this.products().find(p =>
      p.id === productId);

    if (product) {
      this.cartService.addProduct(product);
    }
  }
}
```

Update the template (Listing 2-6) using the newly provided Signals by calling them as functions.

Listing 2-6. Updating the Home Component Template

```
<!-- src/app/pages/home/home.component.html -->

@if (loading()) {
  <p>Loading products...</p>
```

```
} @else {
  <h2>Products in catalog: {{ products().length }}</h2>
  <p>Items in cart: {{ cartCount() }}</p>

  @for (product of products(); track product.id) {
    <div style="margin-bottom: 1rem;">
      <strong>{{ product.title }}</strong> -
        ${{ product.price | currency}}

      <button (click)="addToCart(product.id)">
        Add to Cart
      </button>
    </div>
  }
}
```

What You Should See in the Browser

If you've followed along and served the application (ng serve), you should now see what is shown in Figure 2-1.

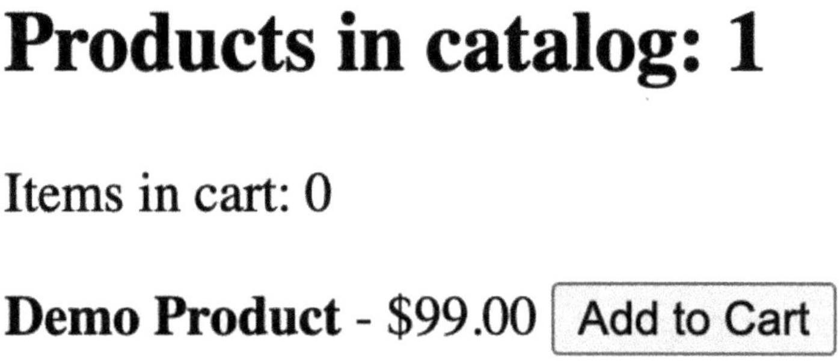

Products in catalog: 1

Items in cart: 0

Demo Product - $99.00 [Add to Cart]

Figure 2-1. *Products in the Catalog*

Clicking "Add to Cart" should

- Immediately increase the item count shown in the "Items in cart" line

- If you click the same button multiple times, the quantity is incremented behind the scenes, though the UI only reflects the total count for now

This interaction is fully reactive

- When the `CartService` updates its internal signal state, the computed `totalItems` signal is recalculated automatically
- Because `cartCount` in `HomeComponent` is a signal too, the UI updates without any manual subscriptions, observables, or change detection triggers

Note This is the power of signals in action: the component doesn't orchestrate updates; it simply reacts to state changes declared elsewhere.

Even though the UI is simple at this point, you've just implemented a reactive state flow that's clean, efficient, and built to scale.

Architectural Note

With two services now managing independent state, `ProductService` and `CartService`, we've laid the groundwork for a scalable, modular application. Each service owns a single slice of state and exposes derived values via `computed()`.

This separation ensures clear boundaries between concerns. It also allows services to evolve independently. For instance, the cart can later support persistence, multi-currency logic, or promo codes, without needing to touch the product logic at all.

We've also ensured the components stay declarative. They do not orchestrate logic; they just display what the signals provide. This inversion of responsibility is a core strength of the signal model.

Summary

We've now connected two key concepts: raw signal state and derived reactive state. By implementing `CartService`, we gave the application its first real data flow: products are listed, cart items are added, and totals are recalculated automatically using `computed()` signals.

We also updated our `HomeComponent` to remain declarative. It doesn't subscribe to anything, manage memory, or perform manual updates. All it does is read from the signals exposed by the services, and Angular handles the rest.

Our application is now even more reactive. Clicking "Add to Cart" updates the UI instantly, powered entirely by reactive signals, with no event subscriptions or manual state syncing.

This chapter marks the start of building a truly reactive architecture: clear data ownership, efficient updates, and no lifecycle complexity. In the next chapter, we'll fetch data from the backend using Angular's new httpResource API and use signals to track loading and error states, still with no manual wiring. We will also move the product list into its own component and finally add some styling to make our UI more appealing.

CHAPTER 3

Effects, APIs, and Async Data with Signals

In the previous chapter, we wired up a reactive cart and modeled a complete local signal-based data flow. That was a useful foundation, but real applications rarely operate in isolation. At some point, the cart needs to talk to the outside world, loading product details from a server, persisting items, or syncing across devices. These operations are inherently asynchronous, and this is where signals really start to show their strength. Now, we are moving into async territory.

Angular's `httpResource()` API, introduced experimentally in v19.2 (and later refined), let's us fetch data with automatic signals for value, `isLoading`, and `error`. This replaces the need for manual signals like #loading and #products and streamlines the entire `async` pipeline.

We'll use this new API to load product data from FakeStore API, a public endpoint that returns mock product catalog data in a format perfect for our use case.

We'll also start using the `effect()` function. This lets us react to changes in signal-based state, for example, logging errors or syncing values to `localStorage`, without wiring up manual subscriptions or lifecycle hooks.

CHAPTER 3   EFFECTS, APIS, AND ASYNC DATA WITH SIGNALS

Folder Structure Update

We are adding one more component in this chapter.

Table 3-1. *Continued src/app Folder Structure*

Folder	Purpose
app/components/product-list	Adds product-list component to list all products

Refactoring ProductService with httpResource()

Let's update our ProductService (Listing 3-1) to use Angular's httpResource() API.

Listing 3-1. Adding httpResource into the Product Service

```
// src/app/services/product.service.ts

import { Injectable, computed, effect } from '@angular/core';
import { httpResource } from '@angular/common/http';
import { Product } from '../models/product.model';

@Injectable({ providedIn: 'root' })
export class ProductService {
  readonly apiResourceRef = httpResource<Product[]>(() =>
  'https://fakestoreapi.com/products');

  readonly products = this.resource.value;
  readonly isLoading = this.resource.isLoading;
  readonly error = this.resource.error;
  readonly count = computed(() =>
    this.products()?.length ?? 0);
```

```
  constructor() {
    effect(() => {
      const err = this.error();
      if (err) {
        console.error('Product load failed:', err);
      }
    });
  }
}
```

In this service, we have removed the hardcoded mock data and used the new `httpResource` function. Additionally, the `setLoading` function was removed as well in favor of the inbuilt `isLoading` signal provided by the resource.

The service is now purely declarative. No `HttpClient` injection, no subscriptions, no `setLoading()` calls. All loading, error, and data state are expressed as signals.

However, under the hood `httpResource` uses the `HttpClient`, so you will need to import `provideHttpClient()` (Listing 3-2) into the `app.config` providers array.

Listing 3-2. Providing the HttpClient to the app.config.ts

```
// src/app/app.config.ts

import {
  ApplicationConfig,
  provideZoneChangeDetection
} from '@angular/core';
```

```
import { provideRouter } from '@angular/router';
import { provideHttpClient } from '@angular/common/http';
import { routes } from './app.routes';

export const appConfig: ApplicationConfig = {
  providers: [
    provideZoneChangeDetection({ eventCoalescing: true }),
    provideRouter(routes),
    provideHttpClient(),
  ],
};
```

What httpResource() Gives You

The httpResource() function returns an object of type HttpResourceRef<T>, which exposes three signals:

- value() – The actual response data
- isLoading() – Whether the request is in progress
- error() – Any error returned during the request

You can use these directly in your components or templates, no need for an async pipe or explicit subscriptions. The httpResource extends the resource function, so if you are using that, then you can use the same properties as well.

A Note on Eagerness

Unlike HttpClient, which returns cold observables – meaning a request is only triggered when you explicitly subscribe –httpResource() is eager. The HTTP call is initiated immediately upon instantiation of the resource (typically when the service is constructed). This design aligns well with declarative architectures but is something to be aware of, especially when the timing of your API calls matters.

CHAPTER 3 EFFECTS, APIS, AND ASYNC DATA WITH SIGNALS

To defer execution, you can parameterize your httpResource() (Listing 3-3) with a signal-based argument. If the signal evaluates undefined or is intentionally left unset at instantiation time, the request will not fire.

Listing 3-3. Using a Query in the http Resource.

```
private query = signal<string | undefined>(undefined);
private productResourceRef = httpResource<Product[]>(() =>
    query() ?
    `/api/products?q=${query()}` :
    undefined);
```

In this setup, the request won't be sent until the query is set – for example: query.set('shoes') is called. This gives you lazy-fetching semantics with declarative syntax.

Sometimes, you may need more control over request timing than httpResource() provides, for instance, waiting for a user action before firing an HTTP request. In those cases, you can wire a signal-based input to a custom resource function. The example in Listing 3-4 shows how to do this using the native fetch() API.

Listing 3-4. Using a Resource API

```
private category = signal<string | undefined>(undefined);

private categoryResourceRef = resource(() => {
  const value = category();
  if (!value) return undefined;

  return fetch(`/api/products?category=${value}`)
    .then(res => res.json());
});
```

This pattern gives you full flexibility over when and how the fetch happens, while still using Angular's `resource()` API explicitly with a request parameter and loader. Listing 3-5 shows a more idiomatic example using the request parameter.

Listing 3-5. Using the Resource API with a Request

```
private id = signal<string | undefined>(undefined);
private productResourceRef = resource({
  request: () => ({ id: this.id() }),
  loader: ({ request }) =>
    fetch(`/api/products/${request.id}`)
    .then(res => res.json())
});
```

This approach separates the reactive dependency (id) from the side-effect logic (fetch), giving you better encapsulation. It also avoids making a request if `id()` is undefined, while still behaving reactively whenever id changes.

Triggering Fetches Reactively

One of the most powerful patterns enabled by `httpResource()` is (Listing 3-6) in **declarative re-fetching**. If your request is based on a signal input, Angular will re-run the fetch whenever the `category` input changes.

Listing 3-6. Using the Resource API with a Request

```
const category = signal('shoes');
const productResourceRef = httpResource<Product[]>(() => {
  return `/api/products?category=${category()}`);
}
```

Calling category.set('shirts') will automatically trigger a re-fetch from the new URL. There's no need to imperatively call reload() – the framework handles it.

This pattern aligns perfectly with features like filter menus, search boxes, and tabbed views, where the query is user-driven and reflected in a reactive signal.

Understanding effect(): Reactive Side Effects Made Simple

Signals are great for holding and deriving state, but sometimes we need to perform side effects when state changes, such as logging, syncing to localStorage.

Whenever any signal inside an effect() changes, the function automatically runs again. You don't need to track dependencies or set up teardown logic, Angular handles that for you (Listing 3-7).

Listing 3-7. Using the Effect Function

```
constructor() {
  effect(() => {
    if (!this.isEmpty()) {
      localStorage.setItem('cart',
        JSON.stringify(this.items()));
    }
  });
}
```

This will automatically sync the cart to localStorage any time its contents change.

> **Note** effect() gives you reactive, memory-safe side effects in one line. Think of it as Angular's built-in answer to side-effect orchestration.

Important Note on effect() and Injection Context

When using Angular's effect(), it's critical to understand that it must be invoked within an *injection context*. This means you cannot freely call effect() from just anywhere in your component lifecycle – not even inside ngOnInit(). If you attempt to do so, Angular will throw a runtime error:

> ERROR RuntimeError: NG0203: effect() can only be used within an injection context such as a constructor, a factory function, a field initializer, or a function used with "runInInjectionContext". Find more at https://angular.dev/errors/NG0203

Why does this happen? Because Angular needs an *active injector* to resolve any dependencies via inject(), and effect() relies on this to correctly hook into the reactive system. This requirement ensures that signals and effects are initialized with access to Angular's dependency injection mechanism.

Solution 1: Use the Constructor

The most common solution is to define your effect() directly in the component as a member or service constructor. Since constructors run within the injection context by default, inject() and effect() will work seamlessly there.

Solution 2: Use runInInjectionContext()

If, for some reason, you need to delay the creation of an effect – for example, until after component initialization – you can use Angular's runInInjectionContext() function. This utility allows you to temporarily re-enter an injection context by specifying the injector to use. Listing 3-8 shows how you can use it inside ngOnInit().

Listing 3-8. Using the Effect Function

```
ngOnInit() {
  runInInjectionContext(this.injector, () => {
    effect(() => {
      const err = this.err();
        if (err) {
          console.error('Product load failed:', err);
        }
    });
  });
}
```

In this example:

1. this.injector refers to the component's injector (you will need to inject the Injector service into the component).

2. The callback inside runInInjectionContext() is now safe to call effect() and even use inject() inside its body if needed.

This approach is especially helpful in advanced scenarios where you need more control over when an effect is created, but it should be used sparingly. For most use cases, the constructor is still the preferred place to create effects in components and services.

Displaying Data with httpResource()

Now that we've covered how to safely use `effect()`, let's move on and integrate `httpResource()` into a functional UI.

We'll begin by creating a new component to render the list of products. This component will receive data via an input bound to a signal, which we'll wire up from the `HomeComponent` using `httpResource()`.

Run the following command to generate the new component under a components folder inside `src/app`:

```
ng generate component components/product-list --standalone
--skip-tests
```

Once generated, update the component template as shown in Listing 3-9.

Listing 3-9. Product List Template

```html
<!-- src/app/components/product-list/product-list.component.
html -->
<div class="product-grid">
  @for (product of products(); track product.id) {
  <div class="product-card">
    <h3>{{ product.title }}</h3>
    <p class="price">{{ product.price | currency}}</p>
    <button (click)="addToCart(product.id)">
      Add to Cart</button>
  </div>
  } @empty {
   <p>No products to display.</p>
}
</div>
```

This template leverages Angular's control flow syntax (@for, @empty) to render content based on the products() signal. If the product list is empty, a fallback message is shown. Otherwise, each product is displayed in a responsive grid layout.

Let's also add some minimal styles to improve the layout and make the product cards visually appealing (Listing 3-10).

Listing 3-10. Product List Stylesheet

```scss
// src/app/components/product-list/product-list.component.scss
.product-grid {
  display: grid;
  gap: 4rem;
  grid-template-columns:
    repeat(auto-fill, minmax(200px, 1fr));
  margin-top: 1rem;
}
.product-card {
  display: flex;
  flex-direction: column;
  justify-content: space-between;
  border: 1px solid #ddd;
  border-radius: 8px;
  padding: 1rem;
  background: white;
  box-shadow: 0 2px 4px rgba(0, 0, 0, 0.05);
  height: 100%;
}
.product-card h3 {
  font-size: 1.1rem;
  margin-bottom: 0.5rem;
}
```

```css
.product-card .price {
  font-weight: bold;
  margin-bottom: 0.5rem;
}

.product-card button {
  background: #1976d2;
  color: white;
  border: none;
  padding: 0.5rem 0.75rem;
  border-radius: 4px;
  cursor: pointer;
}

.product-card button:hover {
  background: #1565c0;
}
```

Now let's wire up the component class to handle the addToCart() logic using CartService (Listing 3-11).

Listing 3-11. Update the Product List Class

```typescript
// src/app/components/product-list/product-list.component.ts

import { CommonModule } from '@angular/common';
import { Component, inject, input } from '@angular/core';
import { Product } from '../../models/product.model';
import { CartService } from '../../services/cart.service';

@Component({
  selector: 'app-product-list',
  standalone: true,
  imports: [CommonModule],
```

```
  templateUrl: './product-list.component.html',
  styleUrls: ['./product-list.component.scss'],
})
export class ProductListComponent {
  #cartService = inject(CartService);
  products = input.required<Product[] | undefined>();

  addToCart(productId: string) {
    const product = this.products()?.find((p) =>
      p.id === productId);

    if (product) {
      This.#cartService.addProduct(product);
    }
  }
}
```

In this class, we're using the new `input` signal-based API to receive products from the parent component. This new syntax provides a reactive, strongly typed alternative to the traditional `@Input()` decorator. We'll dive deeper into `input` and other component inputs in Chapter 4.

Connecting the HomeComponent

With the `ProductListComponent` in place, we now update the `HomeComponent` to consume the signal data returned by `httpResource()` and delegate display to our new component (Listing 3-12).

Listing 3-12. Update the Home Component Template

```
<!-- src/app/components/product-list/product-list.component.html -->

@if (error(); as err) {
  <p class="error">Error loading products:
```

CHAPTER 3 EFFECTS, APIS, AND ASYNC DATA WITH SIGNALS

```
    {{ err }}
  </p>
} @else if (loading()) {
  <div class="loader"></div>
} @else if (!productsList() ||
    productsList()?.length === 0) {
  <p>No products found.</p>
} @else {
  <h2>Products in catalog: {{ productsList()?.length }}</h2>
  <p>Items in cart: {{ cartCount() }}</p>
  <app-product-list [products]="productsList()" />
}
```

This template cleanly separates each state of the data flow:

- If there's an error, show the error message.
- If the request is loading, show a loading indicator.
- If the result is empty, show a fallback message.
- Otherwise, render the `ProductListComponent`.

Let's now look at the updated `HomeComponent` (Listing 3-13) class that powers this template.

Listing 3-13. Update the Home Component Class

```
// src/app/pages/home/home.component.ts

import { CommonModule } from '@angular/common';
import {
  ChangeDetectionStrategy,
  Component,
  inject
} from '@angular/core';
```

```
import { ProductListComponent } from '../../components/product-
list/product-list.component';
import { ProductService } from '../../services/product.
service';
import { CartService } from '../../services/cart.service';

@Component({
  selector: 'app-home',
  standalone: true,
  imports: [CommonModule, ProductListComponent],
  templateUrl: './home.component.html',
  changeDetection: ChangeDetectionStrategy.OnPush,
})
export class HomeComponent {
  #productService = inject(ProductService);
  #cartService = inject(CartService);

  productsList = this.#productService.products;
  cartCount = this.#cartService.totalItems;

  loading = this.#productService.isLoading;
  error = this.#productService.error;
}
```

What's powerful here is that we didn't write a single subscribe()/async or manual loading/error check in the component class. If you have not used these before, don't worry about it for now. Everything is driven by signals behind the scenes – httpResource() automatically updates the bound signals for loading, error, and data. When the data arrives, Angular updates the DOM reactively. No *ngIf chains. No lifecycle micromanagement. Just declarative templates.

This is the signal-based data flow in action – and we're only scratching the surface.

Working with External APIs

The FakeStore API returns data as seen in Listing 3-14.

Listing 3-14. FakeStore API Data

```
[{
  "id": 1,
  "title": "Fjallraven - Foldsack No. 1 Backpack",
  "price": 109.95,
  "description": "...",
  "category": "men's clothing",
  "image": "https://fakestoreapi.com/img/81fPKd-2AYL._AC_
  SL1500_.jpg"
}]
```

For now, we're only using id, title, and price, but we'll extend our Product model later to support fields like category and rating.

NgRx Effects vs. Signal Effects

In NgRx, side effects refer to any logic that reaches outside the store's pure state management, for example, making an HTTP request, persisting to `localStorage`, or logging errors. NgRx provides `createEffect()` to handle these cases in an isolated, testable way. However, performing such a side effect (Listing 3-15) requires boilerplate.

Listing 3-15. NgRx Effects Comparison

```
loadProducts$ = createEffect(() =>
  this.actions$.pipe(
    ofType(loadProducts),
    switchMap(() =>
      this.http.get('/products').pipe(
```

CHAPTER 3 EFFECTS, APIS, AND ASYNC DATA WITH SIGNALS

```
      map(products => loadProductsSuccess({ products })),
      catchError(err => of(loadProductsFailure({
      error: err })))
    )
   )
  )
);
```

This pattern gives you control and traceability, but at the cost of cognitive load, testing complexity, and verbosity.

With Signals, the same intent becomes declarative and local (Listing 3-16).

Listing 3-16. Signal Effects

```
constructor() {
  effect(() => {
    const err = this.error();
    if (err) {
      console.error('Product load failed:', err);
    }
  });
}
```

There's no dispatching, piping, teardown, or isolation ceremony. Signals are tracked automatically, and Angular knows when to re-run your code.

Architectural Note

The httpResource() API marks a meaningful shift in how Angular manages asynchronous data. Unlike HttpClient, which returns an Observable and leaves it to the developer to manage its lifecycle, httpResource() provides a **signal-native interface** for working with remote data.

It cleanly abstracts away loading, error, and value handling, and exposes a reactive surface that integrates directly with template control flow (@if, @for), or computed state. Combined with effect(), you get powerful orchestration without boilerplate.

This is Angular's first asynchronous API designed specifically for Signals. The removal of teardown logic, manual loading flags, and lifecycle noise makes it a natural fit for signal-driven architectures.

Even though it's currently marked as experimental, its ergonomics and composability make it more expressive and maintainable than traditional RxJS-driven flows.

What You Should See in the Browser

If you serve the app now (ng serve), you'll see Figure 3-1.

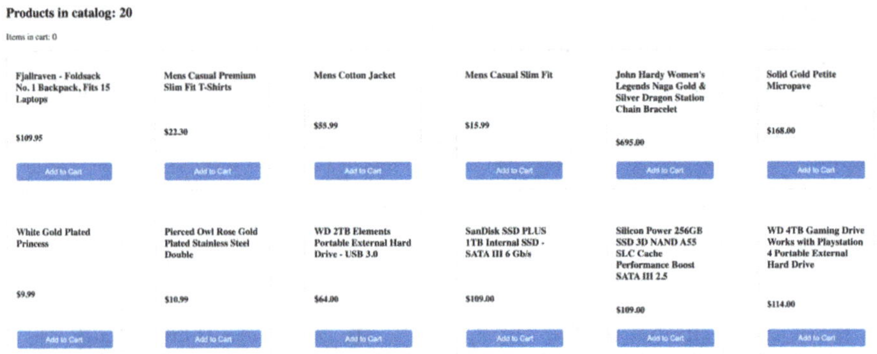

Figure 3-1. List of Products

- A loading message briefly appears
- A list of products listed from the FakeStore API
- A line showing: "Items in cart: 0"

CHAPTER 3   EFFECTS, APIS, AND ASYNC DATA WITH SIGNALS

- Clicking "Add to Cart" will immediately update the count
- If the API fails, you'll see a red error message

Behind the scenes, signals update automatically, and the view reacts without subscriptions or manual orchestration. The `effect()` in `ProductService` logs any load errors without needing to subscribe to anything.

Summary

In this chapter, we replaced manual loading logic with a fully reactive `httpResource()` integration. By switching from imperative orchestration to declarative signals, we dramatically reduced boilerplate and improved clarity.

We also introduced `effect()`, a powerful tool for running side effects when signals change. Effects replace the need for manual subscriptions or external lifecycle handling, making patterns like logging, syncing, and auto-fetching intuitive and safe.

To underscore the simplicity, we compared this to NgRx effects, which require boilerplate-heavy setup. In contrast, Signals allow reactive side effects to be written inline - with automatic dependency tracking and cleanup.

With these tools in place, the app is now powered by fully declarative state and async logic, setting the stage for sharing reactive data across deeply nested components in the next chapter.

CHAPTER 4

Component Communication with Signals

As applications grow, state and logic often need to be shared between components: parents and children, siblings, or deeply nested views. In traditional Angular applications, this has typically involved `@Input()`, `@Output()`, shared services, or `EventEmitter`.

In a Signals-first architecture, we still use services to share state, but the mechanics of communication are far simpler. Signals give us an always-fresh, read-only view of the current state. Components can read from signals declaratively, and re-render when needed.

Signals transform component communication from an imperative push model to a declarative pull model. Instead of asking, "How do I notify X about Y?", we ask, "What state does this component reflect?" If that state is represented as a signal, Angular takes care of the rest.

In this chapter, we'll explore two common patterns:

1. *Parent–child communication*: Where a child component consumes a shared service injected into both components.

2. *Sibling communication*: Where components respond to changes in a common reactive source.

We'll also clarify when it makes sense to pass signals explicitly via inputs, and when to rely on service injection.

Folder Structure Update

In this chapter, we are going to add the HeaderComponent (Table 4-1).

Table 4-1. *Continued src/app Folder Structure*

Folder	Purpose
app/components/header	Adds header component to show a count of items in the cart and the total price

Creating a Shared Cart Header Component

Let's begin by creating a HeaderComponent that shows the current number of items in the cart. This is not a child of HomeComponent, but rather a persistent layout element that could appear on every page.

We'll place it into the app/components folder. Run the following command in your terminal.

```
npx ng generate component components/header --standalone --skip-tests
```

CHAPTER 4   COMPONENT COMMUNICATION WITH SIGNALS

This section demonstrates the **second communication pattern** introduced earlier: **sibling components reacting to shared state**. The HeaderComponent and HomeComponent don't talk to each other directly - instead, they both consume the reactive CartService. This allows them to stay in sync without coupling.

Add the code from Listing 4-1 into the component class.

Listing 4-1. Header Component Class

```
// src/app/components/header/header.component.ts

@Component({
...
})
export class HeaderComponent {
  private readonly cartService = inject(CartService);

  readonly totalItems = this.cartService.totalItems;
  readonly totalPrice = this.cartService.totalPrice;
}
```

Then update the template (Listing 4-2).

Listing 4-2. Header Component Template

```
// src/app/components/header/header.component.html

<header class="header">
  <a routerLink="/">Shop</a>

  <div class="header-actions">
    🛒 {{ totalItems() }} items -
    {{ totalPrice() | currency }}
  </div>
</header>
```

And add the styles (Listing 4-3).

Listing 4-3. Header Component Styles

```scss
// src/app/components/header/header.component.scss
.header {
  display: flex;
  justify-content: space-between;
  align-items: center;
  padding: 1rem;
  background: #1976d2;
  color: white;
}
a {
  color: white;
  text-decoration: none;
}
.header-actions {
  display: flex;
  align-items: center;
  gap: 1rem;
}
```

This component is completely decoupled from HomeComponent, yet it reacts to cart changes automatically. The header doesn't need to subscribe or emit anything. It simply reads from signals, and Angular re-renders it when the signal values change.

Since we are now rendering the count in the header, we can go ahead and remove `<p>Items in cart: {{ cartCount() }}</p>` from our home component template.

Rendering the Header in the Shell

We'll now update AppComponent to include (Listing 4-4) this header above the router outlet.

Listing 4-4. Updating the app component

```
// src/app/app.component.ts

import { Component } from '@angular/core';
import { RouterOutlet } from '@angular/router';
import { HeaderComponent } from './header/header.component';
@Component({
  selector: 'app-root',
  standalone: true,
  imports: [RouterOutlet, HeaderComponent],
  template: `
    <app-header />
    <router-outlet />
  `
})
export class AppComponent {}
```

The HeaderComponent now renders above every routed view (Figure 4-1). Since it reads from a shared signal, any component that modifies the cart will cause the header to update automatically. There's no manual wiring – just reactive state, declaratively consumed.

CHAPTER 4   COMPONENT COMMUNICATION WITH SIGNALS

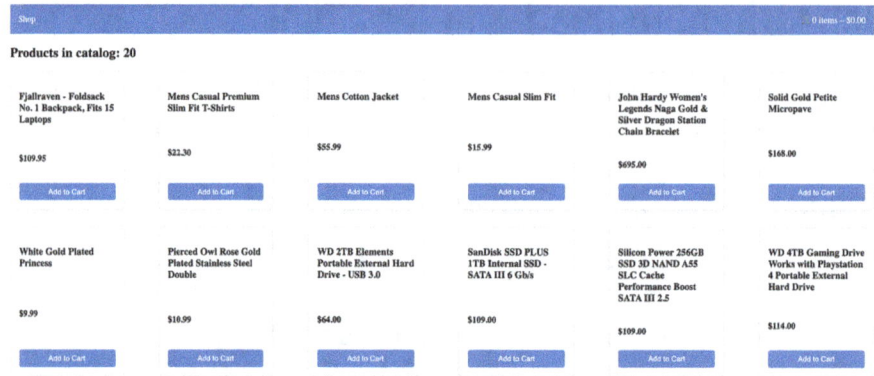

Figure 4-1. The New Products Page

Passing Signals to Child Components

Earlier in Chapter 3, we introduced the `ProductListComponent` and used the new signal-based `input` API to receive a list of products. This modern alternative to `@Input()` gives us strongly typed, reactive bindings – no decorators or manual tracking needed.

Now let's return to that example to highlight the first communication pattern from our introduction: parent-child communication via explicit signal inputs.

Sometimes you'll want to pass a signal directly to a child component – especially when the data is contextual or tied to a specific page. This keeps the child component stateless, testable, and focused on rendering, without requiring it to inject a service.

Listing 4-5 shows how we pass the signal to `ProductListComponent` in `HomeComponent`.

Listing 4-5. Passing a Signal Input to a Child

```html
<!-- src/app/pages/home/home.component.html -->

<h2>Products</h2>
<app-product-list [products]="products()" />
```

And the input is declared using the signal-based API (Listing 4-6).

Listing 4-6. Input Declaration

```typescript
// src/app/components/product-list/product-list.component.ts

export class ProductListComponent {
  products = input.required<Product[] | undefined>();
}
```

This simple pattern keeps reactivity intact while giving the parent full control over what data is passed in. Whenever the products signal in the parent updates, Angular automatically re-evaluates the child template.

This style of communication is especially useful when

- The data is specific to a particular page or context.

- You want to test the child component independently without mocking services.

- You're avoiding unnecessary shared services for data that doesn't need to be global.

By passing the signal directly, we preserve encapsulation without sacrificing reactivity.

This approach is ideal when you want to keep logic encapsulated in a parent but delegate rendering to child components, without sacrificing reactivity or testability.

CHAPTER 4   COMPONENT COMMUNICATION WITH SIGNALS

> **WHEN TO USE SIGNAL INPUTS VS SERVICE INJECTION?**
>
> Both signal inputs and service injection are valid ways to share state between components. The key is knowing when to use each.
>
> Use Signal Inputs when:
>
> - The data is contextual (e.g., filtered products, selected tab, per-page state).
> - The child shouldn't depend on any specific service.
> - You want to unit-test the component in isolation.
> - The component is meant to be highly reusable and flexible.
>
> Use Service Injection when:
>
> - The data is application-wide (e.g., cart state, auth state).
> - The component needs access to shared logic (e.g., methods like addToCart()).
> - Multiple components need to stay in sync without being tightly coupled.
> - You want to avoid passing multiple signals through several layers of the tree.
>
> By combining these two patterns, you can keep your components focused, testable, and clean – all while enjoying the power of Signals.

Architectural Note

Angular Signals allow you to rethink component communication as reactive consumption, not imperative messaging. Instead of pushing data through @Input()/@Output() bindings or Subject streams, components simply consume signals, and Angular handles updates automatically.

The big shift here is that state changes don't need to be "announced". If a component depends on a signal, it will react. If it doesn't, it won't be "announced".

Signals also remove the need for shared `BehaviorSubjects`, manual change detection, or event emitters. Components become observers of state, not managers of it. And because `Signal<T>` is a first-class type, you can explicitly pass it into a child and still benefit from type inference, reactivity, and testability.

This simplifies architecture, reduces boilerplate, and helps you avoid prop drilling altogether.

Comparison Note: Without Signals

In a traditional Angular application without Signals, component communication typically involves

- `@Input()` bindings for passing data down
- `@Output()` emitters for notifying parents of changes
- Shared services with `BehaviorSubject` or `ReplaySubject` for sibling communication
- Manual `ChangeDetectorRef.markForCheck()` calls in OnPush components
- Boilerplate `ngOnDestroy()` logic to unsubscribe from observables

Listings 4-7 and 4-8 show how this would look using `BehaviorSubject` and manual subscriptions.

Listing 4-7. Example Using BehaviorSubject in a Service

```
// cart.service.ts (non-signal)

#totalItems = new BehaviorSubject<number>(0);
readonly totalItems$ = this.#totalItems.asObservable();
addProduct(p: Product) {
  // logic ...
  this.#totalItems.next(newCount);
}
```

The component would subscribe and manage cleanup.

Listing 4-8. Component Using the Above Service

```
ngOnInit() {
  this.subscription = this.#cartService.totalItems$
    .subscribe(
      count => this.cartCount = count
    );
}

ngOnDestroy() {
  this.subscription.unsubscribe();
}
```

Signals eliminate complexity, reduce noise, and make state communication feel native, not bolted on.

Summary

In this chapter, we connected multiple components to a shared state using Angular Signals, without a single subscription or event emitter. We built a HeaderComponent that reacts to cart state globally and a ProductListComponent that accepts a Signal<Product[]> from its parent.

CHAPTER 4   COMPONENT COMMUNICATION WITH SIGNALS

Signals allowed us to fully decouple UI rendering from state management. Whether injected via service or passed explicitly via `input`, Signals act as self-updating streams of truth that components can rely on.

This change is subtle but powerful. Components are no longer "informed" of state changes; they simply reflect them. That inversion of control leads to less code, fewer bugs, and a more declarative mental model.

In the next chapter, we'll explore how routing and guards can also benefit from signal-driven patterns, such as showing different routes depending on login state or guarding access to the checkout page based on cart contents.

CHAPTER 5

Routing, Guards, and Auth with Signals

Routing is at the heart of any Angular application. It determines which components render for which URLs and provides crucial lifecycle entry points for controlling user flow and enforcing access policies. Traditionally, route guards, authentication flows, and UI updates based on login state are implemented using services and observables. While functional, this pattern can become noisy and error-prone, especially when handling async state.

In this chapter (Table 5-1), we'll explore how Angular Signals can simplify routing logic:

- Declaratively guarding access to routes like /checkout
- Reactively updating the UI when the user logs in or out
- Using signals to derive navigation state in a fully declarative way

By the end of this chapter, your UI should look similar to Figure 5-1.

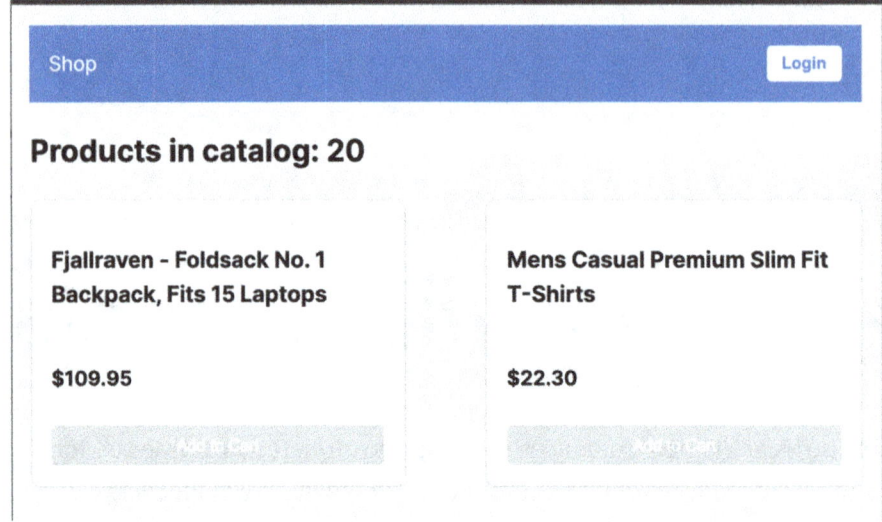

Figure 5-1. UI Update Showing the New Header Components

Folder Structure Update

Table 5-1. Continued src/app Folder Structure

Folder	Purpose
app/services/auth.service.ts	Add a new authentication service
app/guards/auth.guard.ts	Add a new authentication guard
src/app/pages/login	New login component
src/app/pages/checkout	New protected checkout component

Creating the Authentication Service

We'll start with a service that tracks authentication status in memory. While a real-world implementation might involve token storage, refresh flows, or backend validation, the architectural shape remains the same.

CHAPTER 5 ROUTING, GUARDS, AND AUTH WITH SIGNALS

At the core of our solution is a single signal that holds the current user's identity (Listing 5-1). From that, we derive whether a user is logged in or not using a computed value. This ensures that any part of the app depending on authentication state can react automatically and precisely when the underlying value changes – without needing to subscribe or manually trigger change detection.

Listing 5-1. Auth Service

```
// src/app/services/auth.service.ts

import { Injectable, signal, computed } from '@angular/core';

@Injectable({ providedIn: 'root' })
export class AuthService {
  #user = signal<string | null>(null);

  readonly isLoggedIn = computed(() =>
    this.#user() !== null);

  readonly username = computed(() =>
    this.#user());

  login(name: string) {
    this.#user.set(name);
  }

  logout() {
    this.#user.set(null);
  }
}
```

Let's walk through what this service actually does:

- `#user`: This private signal holds the name of the logged-in user, or null if no one is logged in.

- `isLoggedIn`: A computed value that returns true if a user is logged in and false otherwise. This is ideal for conditionally rendering components or protecting routes.

- `username`: A computed signal that gives access to the current user's name. Useful for displaying personalized greetings or audit information.

- `login(name)`: A simple method that sets the user signal to a non-null value.

- `logout()`: Clears the user state by setting it back to null.

This small service is a perfect example of how signals shine in state encapsulation. Everything is reactive out of the box. Any component that reads from `isLoggedIn` or `username` will automatically update when login state changes, without any subscriptions or manual teardown. It's a much cleaner alternative to the typical `BehaviorSubject` or `ReplaySubject` based auth services found in many Angular apps.

In the sections that follow, we'll see how to wire this service into the router and the UI in a clean, declarative fashion.

Creating a Login Page

We now scaffold a login screen. In this example, it simply calls `auth.login()` and redirects. This can be replaced with a full authentication form later.

```
npx ng generate component pages/login --standalone --skip-tests
```

CHAPTER 5   ROUTING, GUARDS, AND AUTH WITH SIGNALS

This LoginComponent (Listing 5-2) demonstrates how to trigger a login action and redirect the user. For now, we hard-code a username to simulate login flow.

Listing 5-2. Login Component

```
// src/app/pages/login/login.component.ts

import { Component, inject } from '@angular/core';
import { CommonModule } from '@angular/common';
import { Router } from '@angular/router';
import { AuthService } from '../../services/auth.service';

@Component({
  selector: 'app-login',
  standalone: true,
  imports: [CommonModule],
  templateUrl: './login.component.html'
})
export class LoginComponent {
  private readonly auth = inject(AuthService);
  private readonly router = inject(Router);

  login() {
    this.auth.login('sonu');
    this.router.navigateByUrl('/');
  }
}

<!-- login.component.html -->

<h2>Login</h2>
<button (click)="login()">Sign In as Sonu</button>
```

This stub shows how signal-powered state integrates with Angular navigation. Once logged in, the user is redirected. Figure 5-2 shows how the login page should look.

Figure 5-2. Login Page

Creating a Checkout Page and Route Guard

To enforce login requirements for sensitive areas of our app, such as the /checkout route, we need to integrate routing with our authentication logic. This is a perfect use case for Angular route guards combined with our reactive AuthService.

We'll walk through the following:

- Creating a new CheckoutComponent
- Writing a route guard that checks login state via a signal
- Applying that guard to a route
- Testing the full login-redirect-checkout flow

Run the following command to generate a standalone checkout page component:

```
ng generate component pages/checkout --standalone --skip-tests
```

Create the Guard

We'll now define a simple route guard (Listing 5-3) using the CanActivateFn syntax. This functional guard checks if the user is logged in by accessing the isLoggedIn computed signal from our AuthService. If the signal returns false, we redirect to /login.

Listing 5-3. Auth Guard

```
// src/app/guards/auth.guard.ts

import { inject } from '@angular/core';
import { CanActivateFn, Router } from '@angular/router';
import { AuthService } from '../services/auth.service';

export const authGuard: CanActivateFn = () => {
  const auth = inject(AuthService);
  const router = inject(Router);

  if (!auth.isLoggedIn()) {
    router.navigateByUrl('/login');
    return false;
  }

  return true;
};
```

Even though we're using signals under the hood, the guard itself executes synchronously. This is intentional – Angular expects guards to return synchronously (or a Promise/Observable). Since our signal state is fully in-memory and synchronous, this integration is seamless.

Protecting the Route

Next, let's apply our guard to the /checkout route (Listing 5-4) by updating the application's route configuration. This ensures that only logged-in users will be allowed to access the CheckoutComponent.

Listing 5-4. Auth Route

```
// src/app/app.routes.ts

import { Routes } from '@angular/router';
import { HomeComponent } from './pages/home/home.component';
import { LoginComponent } from './pages/login/login.component';
import { CheckoutComponent } from './pages/checkout/checkout.component';
import { authGuard } from './guards/auth.guard';

export const routes: Routes = [
  { path: '', component: HomeComponent },
  { path: 'login', component: LoginComponent },
  { path: 'checkout',
    component: CheckoutComponent,
    canActivate: [authGuard]
  }
];
```

Takeaway: Because authGuard reads from a computed signal (isLoggedIn()), the route configuration remains simple and declarative, while the logic remains reactive and testable.

A Minimal Checkout View

Now let's provide a minimal implementation (Listing 5-5) for the checkout view. We will change the HTML later.

Listing 5-5. Checkout Component

```
<!-- checkout.component.html -->

<h2>Checkout Page</h2>
<p>You must be logged in to access this page.</p>
```

This gives us a complete example to confirm login-based navigation works as expected.

Try It Yourself

To see it in action:

1. Run the app using ng serve
2. Navigate to the protected route
3. Open http://localhost:4200/checkout in your browser.
4. You should be redirected to /login because you're not logged in yet.
5. Trigger a login
6. Click "Sign in as Sonu" button (we'll wire this up later in the UI).
7. Post-login redirection

CHAPTER 5   ROUTING, GUARDS, AND AUTH WITH SIGNALS

  8. You should be taken to the homepage.

  9. Try /checkout again

  10. Now when you visit /checkout, you should see the message from Listing 5-5.

This flow demonstrates the power of using Angular Signals for routing state. Even though route guards themselves are synchronous, they can safely read from reactive state like auth.isLoggedIn (see Listing 5-1), as long as that state is stable and synchronous.

There's no need for asynchronous guards, observable subscriptions, or manually tracking login events. Signals let us model authentication status in a way that's declarative, encapsulated, and easy to reason about across both routing and UI layers.

In the next section, we'll reactively show or hide UI elements like navigation links and buttons based on this same login state.

Controlling Access to Cart Actions

At this point, your application correctly guards the /checkout route for logged-in users. But there's still an inconsistency: a logged-out user can still click **"Add to Cart"** and interact with the shopping flow – only to lose their cart contents when they log in.

To make this flow coherent and predictable, we'll disable (Listing 5-6) the **Add to Cart** button unless the user is logged in. This gives clear visual feedback and prevents accidental state loss.

Listing 5-6. Product List Component Template Update

```
<!-- src/app/components/product-list/product-list.component.html -->
...
<button
```

```
  (click)="addToCart(product.id)"
  [disabled]="!isLoggedIn()">
  Add to Cart
</button>
```

Listing 5-7. Product List Component Class Update

```
...
@Component({
...
})
export class ProductListComponent {
...
  #authService = inject(AuthService);

  readonly isLoggedIn = this.#authService.isLoggedIn;
}
```

Here, isLoggedIn (Listing 5-7) is the same computed signal shown in Listing 5-1. Angular templates automatically respond to signal changes, so once the user logs in, the button will re-enable without needing any manual wiring.

For completeness, let's also update the styles (Listing 5-8).

Listing 5-8. Product List Component Class Update

```
// src/app/components/product-list/product-list.component.scss

.product-card button {
  ...
  &:disabled {
    background: #e0e0e0;
    cursor: not-allowed;
  }
```

CHAPTER 5   ROUTING, GUARDS, AND AUTH WITH SIGNALS

```
  transition: background 0.3s ease;
}

.product-card button:hover:not(:disabled) {
  background: #1565c0;
}
```

> This small tweak ensures consistency between what users can do and what their login state allows – a key aspect of good UX.

With both route access and cart interactions aligned with `isLoggedIn`, your app now has a clean, declarative foundation for access control.

Updating the Header to Show Auth State

Let's update the `HeaderComponent` (Listing 5-9) to reflect whether a user is logged in. We expose both `username` and `isLoggedIn` as signals, and provide a `logout()` method. Notice how we also import the `RouterLink` to ensure that routing is working as expected.

Listing 5-9. Header Component Class Update

```
// src/app/components/header/header.component.ts (additions)

...
import { Router, RouterLink } from '@angular/router';
import { AuthService } from '../../services/auth.service';
import { CartService } from '../../services/cart.service';

@Component({
  ...
})
```

CHAPTER 5 ROUTING, GUARDS, AND AUTH WITH SIGNALS

```
export class HeaderComponent {
  #cart = inject(CartService);
  #auth = inject(AuthService);
  #router = inject(Router);

  readonly totalItems = this.#cart.totalItems;
  readonly totalPrice = this.#cart.totalPrice;
  readonly isEmpty = this.#cart.isEmpty;

  readonly username = this.#auth.username;
  readonly isLoggedIn = this.#auth.isLoggedIn;

  logout() {
    this.#auth.logout();
    this.#router.navigateByUrl('/');
  }
}
```

What's happening here:

- All signals from both AuthService and CartService are exposed directly to the class.
- No subscriptions, no manual state management.
- The logout() method clears the auth state and routes back to the homepage.

The template in Listing 5-10 now conditionally shows a welcome message and logout button if a user is logged in. Otherwise, it displays a login button.

Listing 5-10. Header Component Template Update

```html
<!-- src/app/components/header/header.component.html -->

<header class="header">
  <a routerLink="/">Shop</a>

  <div class="header-actions">
    @if (!isEmpty()) {
      🛒 {{ totalItems() }} items -
      {{ totalPrice() | currency }}
    } @if (isLoggedIn()) {
      <span class="user-info">
        👤 {{ username() }}
      </span>
      <button class="auth-button"
        (click)="logout()">Logout
      </button>
    } @else {
      <button class="auth-button"
        routerLink= "/login">
        Login
      </button>
    }
  </div>
</header>
```

The header is now fully reactive. It reflects username and `isLoggedIn`, both of which are signals. When login state changes, the UI updates without wiring.

We also added the CSS (Listing 5-11) classes to keep the layout clean and accessible.

Listing 5-11. Header Component CSS Styles Update

```scss
// src/app/components/header/header.component.scss

.cart-button,
.auth-button {
  background: white;
  color: #1976d2;
  border: none;
  padding: 0.4rem 0.75rem;
  font-weight: bold;
  border-radius: 4px;
  cursor: pointer;
}

.cart-button:hover,
.auth-button:hover {
  background: #e3e3e3;
}

.user-info {
  font-size: 0.9rem;
  margin-right: 0.5rem;
}
```

And finally, we added the font style in Listing 5-12 into our global styles.scss.

Listing 5-12. Global Styles Class Update

```scss
body {
  font-family: "Inter", sans-serif;
  font-size: 16px;
  line-height: 1.5;
  color: #222;
```

```
  margin: 0;
  background: #f9f9f9;
  padding: 1rem;
}
```

Figure 5-3 shows how this should look once the user is logged in and Figure 5-4 shows how this looks when the user has products added to their cart.

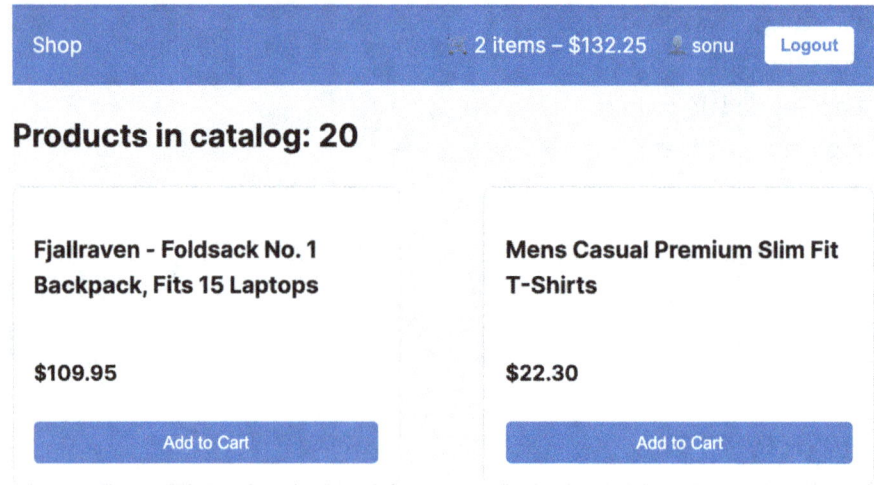

Figure 5-3. *After Login*

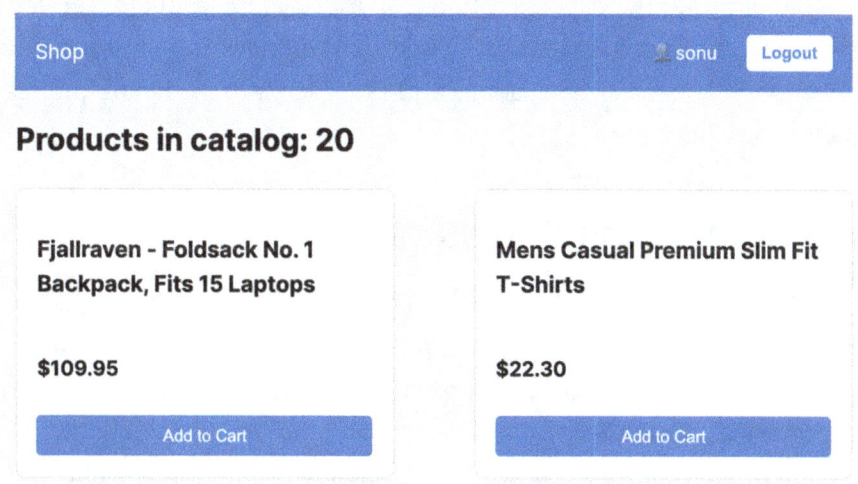

Figure 5-4. *Products Added to the Cart*

Architectural Note

While we've used a simple login model here, the implications are significant when comparing to other state management strategies like NgRx.

Why This Is Cleaner Than NgRx

NgRx-based route guards require selectors, effectful stores, and coordination between dispatched actions and subscribed state. A typical guard might wait on a store selector with `take(1)`, or filter, then resolve a promise.

With signals, the guard simply reads from a computed value. That synchronous call is derived from reactive state, meaning it always reflects the latest truth – no observable orchestration or manual memory management involved.

More importantly, the integration with routing and layout is seamless. Instead of using `Store.select(...)` in the component and piping into an async pipe, you can use `username()` and `isLoggedIn()` as signals and read directly from them.

What About Signal Routers?

At the time of writing, the Angular team has acknowledged that Signal-based routing is on the roadmap. Future APIs may allow for first-class signal-powered navigation guards, reactive route resolution, and dynamic component rendering.

Until then, what we've shown here is already usable, lightweight, and aligns well with Angular's current APIs. Everything from the `inject()` powered guard to the signal-based layout rendering is future-compatible.

Why This Matters in the Real World

Imagine a user login state controlling not just route access, but conditional menu visibility, remote role checks, and active route highlighting – all based on signals. With computed derivation, you get consistent state updates across route guards, UI components, and service logic without coupling or imperative glue code.

The result is less error-prone, more readable, and drastically easier to test.

Signals and routing integrate cleanly. Route guards that previously relied on observables or async logic now consume computed values directly.

This represents a subtle but significant shift: your access model becomes a pure projection of reactive state. Guard logic is no longer wrapped in `pipe()`, `map()`, or async callbacks – it's synchronous in syntax, but reactive in effect.

CHAPTER 5   ROUTING, GUARDS, AND AUTH WITH SIGNALS

Using signals also improves **testability** and reduces risk of race conditions or delayed navigation flows.

Moreover, reflecting auth state in layout components like headers becomes trivial. There's no coordination layer. Every component that consumes a signal gets real-time access to the current application state.

This pattern scales naturally:

- Protect admin routes based on user.role

- Show onboarding banners if user.hasCompletedIntro() is false

- Derive UI routes based on feature flags, permissions, or even cart().length

Summary

In this chapter, we

- Created an AuthService that tracks user identity using signals

- Built a LoginComponent for sign-in flow

- Guarded the /checkout route using a signal-driven route guard

- Updated the HeaderComponent to reflect login status reactively

We avoided subscriptions, event emitters, or async streams – and instead relied on signals to make routing declarative and composable.

This sets the stage for building deeply interactive Angular apps where routing, layout, and UI state all flow from the same reactive core.

In the next chapter, we'll turn our attention to testing, debugging, and performance: how to inspect and test signals, when to use effect(), and how to push performance even further using zone-less rendering.

CHAPTER 6

Testing, Debugging, and Performance Tuning

Angular Signals don't just change how we model reactivity – they also reshape how we test and debug applications. With their synchronous nature, dependency tracking, and predictable behavior, Signals make it easier to validate service logic, write reactive UI tests, and inspect application state as it evolves.

In this chapter, we'll walk through how to test services that use signals and effect(), how to validate component behavior when signals change, and how Angular DevTools now gives us deep insight into reactive flows. We'll also close with some best practices that will help keep your signal architecture robust and maintainable as your application grows.

Why We Skipped Tests Until Now

Earlier in the book, we intentionally skipped generating test files when scaffolding components and services. At that point, our focus was on building features and learning how Signals work. Introducing Angular's default testing scaffolding too early would have brought unnecessary complexity before readers fully understood the patterns being tested.

Now, with a solid understanding of signal-first architecture, we're in a better position to appreciate how elegantly Signals fit into the testing workflow.

Folder Structure Update

In this chapter, we are going to add the tests (Table 6-1). Go ahead and create these files manually.

Table 6-1. Continued src/app Folder Structure

Folder	Purpose
app/services/cart.service.spec.ts	Add a spec file for the cart service
app/components/header/header.component.spec.ts	Add a spec file for the header component

Writing Tests for Signal-Based Services

Unlike observables, signals are synchronous and behave like simple, trackable function calls. There's no need for subscriptions, teardown logic, or async wrappers like `fakeAsync`. Testing signal-based state becomes a matter of evaluating values and asserting outcomes – almost like testing plain functions.

To explore this, we'll revisit our `CartService`. It holds cart items in a signal, derives totals using `computed()`, and uses an `effect()` to persist cart changes to `localStorage`. All of this can be tested deterministically.

When testing a service that includes `effect()`, it must be instantiated through Angular's dependency injection system using `TestBed`. This is because `effect()` requires an injection context to function (See Chapter 3 for more on effects). If we try to create the service directly using new, we'll encounter Angular's NG0203 error.

CHAPTER 6 TESTING, DEBUGGING, AND PERFORMANCE TUNING

NG0203: effect() can only be used within an injection context such as a constructor, a factory function, a field initializer, or a function used with runInInjectionContext. Find more at https://angular.dev/errors/NG0203

Listing 6-1 shows how we set up the test environment.

Listing 6-1. Cart Service Test Setup

```
// src/app/services/cart.service.spec.ts

let service: CartService;

beforeEach(() => {
  TestBed.configureTestingModule({
    providers: [CartService]
  });

  service = TestBed.inject(CartService);
  spyOn(localStorage, 'setItem');
});
```

This setup gives us a clean instance of the service and allows us to spy on the localStorage.setItem() method so we can assert that our effect executed correctly.

Now let's walk through some tests.

The first test (Listing 6-2) ensures that when a product is added to the cart, the internal signal reflects the correct item count and the effect() triggers a write to localStorage.

CHAPTER 6   TESTING, DEBUGGING, AND PERFORMANCE TUNING

Listing 6-2. Test Add a Product

```
it('adds a product and persists to localStorage', () => {
  const product: Product = {
    id: 'p1',
    title: 'Laptop',
    price: 1200,
  };

  service.addProduct(product);
  TestBed.tick();

  expect(service.totalItems()).toBe(1);
  expect(localStorage.setItem).toHaveBeenCalledWith(
    'cart',
    JSON.stringify([{ product, quantity: 1 }])
  );
});
```

In this case, the `effect()` is triggered after the cart changes, but Angular defers it slightly in tests. This is why we call `TestBed.tick()` – it ensures that all queued effects are executed before we make assertions.

In the next test (Listing 6-3), we confirm that clearing the cart resets the item count and persists an empty array to storage. This verifies that destructive updates are also fully reactive.

Listing 6-3. Clear the Cart Test

```
it('clears the cart and persists an empty array', () => {
  const product: Product = {
    id: 'abc',
    title: 'Signal Hoodie',
    price: 65,
  };
```

CHAPTER 6 TESTING, DEBUGGING, AND PERFORMANCE TUNING

```
  service.addProduct(product);
  service.clear();
  TestBed.tick();

  expect(service.totalItems()).toBe(0);
  expect(service.items()).toEqual([]);
  expect(localStorage.setItem).
  toHaveBeenCalledWith('cart', '[]');
});
```

We're not just checking internal state here – we're validating that the application persisted that state externally through a side-effect. This kind of test is common when working with services that must synchronize with storage, analytics, or the network.

One more scenario (Listing 6-4) we should test is removing a product from the cart. This test confirms that the cart updates correctly and that the persisted state reflects the change.

Listing 6-4. Remove a Product Test

```
it('removes a product and persists the updated cart', () => {
  const product: Product = {
    id: 'abc',
    title: 'Signal Hoodie',
    price: 65,
  };

  service.addProduct(product);
  service.removeProduct(product.id);
  TestBed.tick();

  expect(service.items()).toEqual([]);
  expect(localStorage.setItem).
  toHaveBeenCalledWith('cart', '[]');
});
```

CHAPTER 6   TESTING, DEBUGGING, AND PERFORMANCE TUNING

Across all three tests, we never deal with observables, subscriptions, or change detection zones. We just drive state, flush effects (through tick), and assert outcomes. That's the power of signals in testing: minimal ceremony, maximum determinism.

Comparing Signal-Based Tests to RxJS-Based Tests

If you've worked with Angular for a while, you're probably familiar with how testing observable-based services can often feel like an uphill battle. Consider this: every interaction with state requires a subscription. And because observables are asynchronous by nature, you're forced to use utilities like fakeAsync, done, or even TestScheduler to manage timing and emissions. Worse yet, forgetting an unsubscribe() can lead to memory leaks or false positives in your tests. Listing 6-5 shows such an example.

Listing 6-5. Typical Observable Based Service Test

```
it('should load products', fakeAsync(() => {
  let products: Product[] = [];

  service.products$.subscribe(p => products = p);

  // emits through an async observable
  service.loadProducts();

  tick(500); // simulate debounce, delay, or network delay

  expect(products.length).toBeGreaterThan(0);
}));
```

This test (Listing 6-5) is fragile: it depends on internal timings, assumes the observable will emit only once, and wraps everything in `fakeAsync()` just to handle what is essentially a synchronous outcome. Every `tick()` must match real-world delays, or the test fails silently or unpredictably.

Some teams try to improve this by using **RxJS marble tests** - which bring in another layer of abstraction and complexity. While powerful, marble syntax is cryptic (`'--a--b|'`, `{ a: value1, b: value2 }`) and hard to debug. Writing and reading marble tests become a specialized skill in itself, especially for new team members.

In contrast, with Signals

- You don't need `subscribe()`. You access state like a getter function.

- You don't need `fakeAsync` or tick. Signals are synchronous and deterministic.

- You don't need to worry about teardown. There's no manual `unsubscribe()`.

- You don't need marbles. Tests reflect actual usage, not an encoded timeline.

This isn't just syntactic sugar - it's a paradigm shift that removes an entire class of boilerplate and gotchas from your test suite.

Testing Signal-Driven Components

Component tests often suffer from verbose setup, complex mocking, and unpredictable change detection. Signals help eliminate much of that. Because they're synchronous and tracked automatically by Angular, signals simplify not only how components respond to state - but how we validate that behavior.

Let's walk through testing the `HeaderComponent`. This component appears at the top of every page and displays the total number of items in the cart. It reads the `totalItems` signal from the `CartService`, which is powered by a signal internally. Every time the cart changes, the signal updates, and the UI re-renders automatically. Listing 6-6 shows our current header component.

Listing 6-6. Simplified Header Component

```html
<!-- src/app/components/header/header.component.html -->
<header class="header">
  <a routerLink="/">Shop</a>
  <div class="header-actions">
  @if (!isEmpty()) {
     🛒 {{ totalItems() }} items -
      {{ totalPrice() | currency }}
  } @if (isLoggedIn()) {
    <span class="user-info">
      👤 {{ username() }}
    </span>
    <button class="auth-button"
      (click)="logout()">Logout
    </button>
  } @else {
    <button class="auth-button"
      routerLink="/login">Login
    </button>
  }
  </div>
</header>
```

CHAPTER 6   TESTING, DEBUGGING, AND PERFORMANCE TUNING

```
...
export class HeaderComponent {
  #cart = inject(CartService);
  #auth = inject(AuthService);
  #router = inject(Router);

  readonly totalItems = this.#cart.totalItems;
  readonly totalPrice = this.#cart.totalPrice;
  readonly isEmpty = this.#cart.isEmpty;

  readonly username = this.#auth.username;
  readonly isLoggedIn = this.#auth.isLoggedIn;

  logout() {
    this.#auth.logout();
    this.#router.navigateByUrl('/');
  }
}
```

This component has no inputs or outputs. It relies entirely on a shared service and tracks reactivity using Signals. We will also be not testing all of its functionality, but rather we will simply check if the header shows a login button when not logged in and the cart item count when the user is logged in.

Let's write a test that validates this behavior. Create the `header.component.spec.ts` file and add the below tests.

Test Setup

Our `TestBed` setup (Listing 6-7) is going to be straightforward. First, we inject the required services and components. Then we get a reference for them. Since the services don't have any additional dependencies and to keep things simple, we are not going to mock them.

CHAPTER 6   TESTING, DEBUGGING, AND PERFORMANCE TUNING

Listing 6-7. TestBed Setup

```
let fixture: ComponentFixture<HeaderComponent>;
let component: HeaderComponent;
let cartService: CartService;
let authService: AuthService;

beforeEach(() => {
  TestBed.configureTestingModule({
    imports: [HeaderComponent],
    providers: [
      CartService,
      AuthService,
      RouterLink,
      {
        provide: ActivatedRoute,
        useValue: {}
      },
    ],
  });

  fixture = TestBed.createComponent(HeaderComponent);
  component = fixture.componentInstance;
  cartService = TestBed.inject(CartService);
  authService = TestBed.inject(AuthService);

  // triggers initial view rendering
  fixture.detectChanges();
});
```

CHAPTER 6 TESTING, DEBUGGING, AND PERFORMANCE TUNING

Test: Should Show a Login Button

In the first test (Listing 6-8), we'll verify that the header shows a login button. This will be the first thing the user sees when they are not logged in. The test's code is self-documenting.

Listing 6-8. Should Show a Login Button Test

```
// src/app/components/header/header.component.spec.ts

it('should show login button when not logged in', () => {
  const header = fixture.nativeElement as HTMLElement;
  const loginButton = header.querySelector(
    'button[routerLink="/login"]'
  );
  expect(loginButton).toBeTruthy();
});
```

Test: Should Display Total Items from the Cart Service Signal

Listing 6-9. Testing the Header Component

```
// src/app/components/header/header.component.spec.ts

it('should display total items
  from CartService signal', () => {

  const header = fixture.nativeElement as HTMLElement;

  authService.login('testuser'); // simulate login
  fixture.detectChanges(); // update the view

  // Initial state: cart is empty
  expect(component.totalItems()).toBe(0);
```

87

CHAPTER 6 TESTING, DEBUGGING, AND PERFORMANCE TUNING

```
  // Mutate state via the service
  cartService.addProduct({
    id: 'p1',
    title: 'Signals Book',
    price: 50,
    imageUrl: '',
  });

  // ensure the view reflects the signal change
  fixture.detectChanges();

  // Updated state: should reflect 1 item
  expect(header.textContent).toContain('1 items');
});
```

In the test shown in Listing 6-9, we're validating not just the state itself, but how it flows into the UI. The test starts by confirming the initial rendered output. It then mutates the cart by adding a product, calls detectChanges(), and finally verifies that the header re-renders with the new count.

This test doesn't require fakeAsync, no whenStable(), and no manual teardown. Signals automatically inform Angular when something changes, and Angular tracks which parts of the view to re-render – all you need to do is tick that change into the DOM using detectChanges().

Even with OnPush change detection, signals take care of view updates because Angular tracks signal accesses in the template. This test proves that reactivity flows through declaratively without subscriptions or event emitters.

CHAPTER 6   TESTING, DEBUGGING, AND PERFORMANCE TUNING

Debugging Signals with Angular DevTools

In Angular v17 and later, the DevTools extension includes first-class support for signals. This makes it easier than ever to understand reactive flows inside your application.

When you inspect a component, the DevTools show

- Each signal the component depends on
- The current value of that signal
- Any computed() chains connected to it
- Which components are re-rendering due to signal changes

To use this, install Angular DevTools (from the Chrome App Store or FireFox Addons), run your app in development mode, and open the **Signals** tab (Figure 6-1) while inspecting a component. You'll gain real-time visibility into how your UI is reacting to state changes.

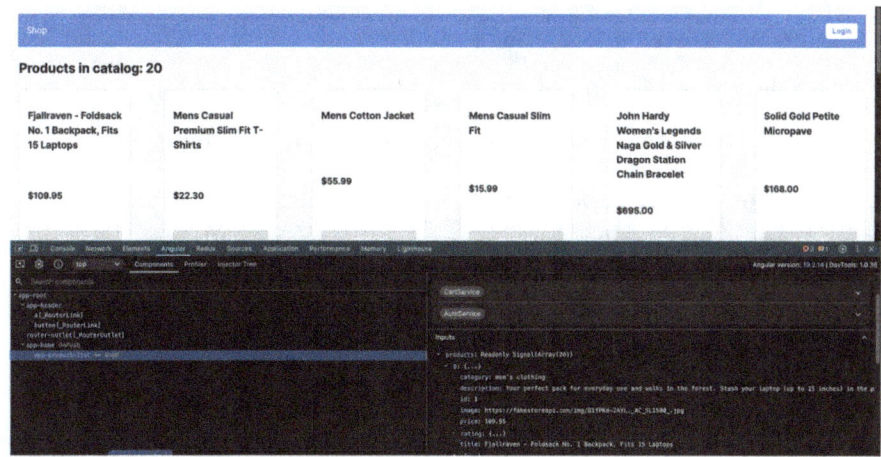

Figure 6-1. Angular Signals Dev Tools

Debugging with Inline Effects

In development, you can also temporarily wire up an `effect()` inside (Listing 6-10) a service or component to trace changes manually. This can be extremely helpful when you're trying to understand whether a signal is being updated as expected, or to confirm which signals are responsible for a downstream computation.

Listing 6-10. Showing an Effect

```
effect(() => {
  console.log('Cart total price:', this.totalPrice());
});
```

This works much like sprinkling `console.log()` inside a `computed` property – but with a crucial difference: it will only run when the signal's dependencies actually change. That means you don't get noisy logs on every change detection pass; you only see logs when the relevant reactive data updates.

Inline effects are particularly useful for

- Tracing derived state - verifying that a computed value such as totalPrice updates correctly as inputs change.

- Confirming dependencies - seeing which signals trigger an update, making it easier to spot accidental dependencies or missing ones.

- Quick sanity checks - dropping an effect into a component or service without setting up a full logger or debugger.

Since `effect()` is part of Angular's reactivity model, you can trust it to fire at the correct time in the update cycle, avoiding false positives you might get from sprinkling logs elsewhere.

> **Caution** Inline effects are best kept as temporary scaffolding. Leaving them in production code can clutter your logs and introduce unnecessary side work. For production-grade debugging or telemetry, consider integrating structured logging or observability tools instead.

Signal Hygiene: Patterns That Scale

Signals are elegant, but elegance fades without discipline. As your app grows, so should your attention be paid to naming, derivation patterns (Listing 6-12), and encapsulation.

Always expose state using asReadonly() (Listing 6-11). This ensures consumers can observe state but cannot mutate it.

Listing 6-11. Use asReadonly

```
#items = signal<CartItem[]>([]);
readonly items = this.#items.asReadonly();
Use computed() for any derived logic. This makes dependencies
explicit and avoids duplicate computation in multiple places.
```

Listing 6-12. Use Computed

```
readonly totalPrice = computed(() =>
  this.items().reduce((sum, item) =>
    sum + item.product.price, 0)
);
```

Avoid large, multi-purpose effect() blocks. Keep them focused on a single responsibility – whether that's persisting in storage, tracking analytics, or navigating the router. This makes effects easier to test and debug.

Finally, name your signals with clarity and intent. These names show up in DevTools, stack traces, and logs, so it pays to be deliberate. Follow these rules when naming signals:

- Be descriptive: Use names that convey domain meaning (`cartItems`, `totalPrice`) rather than vague mechanics (data, value).

- Avoid noise: Skip prefixes like `_signal` or `state`; the fact that it's a signal is already clear from context.

- Reflect usage, not storage: Name signals after what they represent (e.g., `selectedProductId`) instead of how they're stored (`currentIndex`).

- Keep consistent: Stick to a consistent style across your app to make logs and DevTools easier to read.

Summary

In this chapter, we explored what it means to test, debug, and maintain applications built with Angular Signals.

We began by testing services that expose reactive state and side effects. You saw how it is possible to write meaningful tests when your service logic is synchronous, trackable, and declarative. With `TestBed.tick()`, we gained precise control over when reactive side effects fire – making it easy to validate both state changes and persistence.

We then shifted to component testing using the real `HeaderComponent` from our app. Instead of mocking inputs or wiring up outputs, the component simply consumed a signal from a service. Our test confirmed that signal changes updated the DOM with zero subscriptions or teardown logic. This is what makes signal-based UI so powerful: reactivity just works, even in tests.

CHAPTER 6   TESTING, DEBUGGING, AND PERFORMANCE TUNING

We also covered how Angular DevTools now supports Signals, giving you full visibility into which signals your components depend on and how they're derived. And finally, we walked through best practices for structuring signals, naming them, and encapsulating them properly for scale.

Testing no longer needs to feel like a chore. With signals, it's faster, simpler, and more aligned with how we actually build apps.

In the next chapter, we'll shift gears and explore how to migrate existing applications – especially those built with RxJS or NgRx – into this new, signal-first model. You'll learn what to keep, what to drop, and how to evolve without rewriting your entire codebase. In Chapter 8, we will then continue with the UI changes.

CHAPTER 7

From RxJS to Signals – Migration and Interoperability

Angular's reactivity story is undergoing a significant evolution. For years, RxJS was the default for handling any kind of dynamic behavior in Angular – whether it was fetching data, reacting to user input, managing application state, or responding to route changes. Now, with the introduction of Signals, developers have a new, more intuitive way of modeling state and reactions.

But this evolution doesn't require a revolution. Most Angular codebases – especially those in production – are deeply entrenched in RxJS, and more specifically in libraries built on top of it, like NgRx.

This chapter addresses one of the most important practical questions for teams adopting Signals: how can we progressively and safely migrate from RxJS heavy patterns, including NgRx, to a Signal-first architecture?

Along the way, we'll also discuss when RxJS is still the right tool, and how to mix Signals into an existing ecosystem without introducing chaos.

CHAPTER 7   FROM RXJS TO SIGNALS – MIGRATION AND INTEROPERABILITY

Working Alongside RxJS

> The first thing to understand is that Signals are not a replacement for RxJS in every domain.

RxJS excels in dealing with time-based streams, user events, WebSocket messages, and other asynchronous data flows. Signals, on the other hand, are primarily a synchronous state primitive.

What Angular gives us, thankfully, is an excellent interop.

You can convert an Observable to a Signal using `toSignal()`, and you can convert a Signal to an Observable using `toObservable()`. These conversions aren't just utilities – they are a strategic bridge that allows teams to adopt Signals incrementally, without rewriting entire services or tearing down existing data flows.

Imagine a component consuming a stream of product data:

```
readonly products = toSignal(this.productService.products$);
```

Or a service providing a signal to legacy code that still expects Observables:

```
readonly products$ = toObservable(this.products);
```

This allows teams to start writing new features using Signals while letting old code continue working as before.

Introducing linkedSignal() – Controlled Bridging with External State

Throughout this book, we've not used the `linkedSignal()` function. That was deliberate.

CHAPTER 7   FROM RXJS TO SIGNALS – MIGRATION AND INTEROPERABILITY

Early on, the goal is to teach Signals in their purest form – focusing on local state, derived computations, and side effects managed through effect(). However, once you begin migrating an RxJS-heavy app, especially one using libraries like NgRx, you start running into real scenarios where you need to tie a Signal to an external Observable in a more sophisticated way than toSignal() can offer.

This is where linkedSignal() becomes invaluable.

Unlike toSignal(), which passively subscribes to an Observable and must be managed manually, linkedSignal() is lifecycle-aware. When used within an Angular injection context, like in a service or component, it automatically handles teardowns, cleanup, and resubscription. This makes it ideal for bridging external data streams into Signals.

Let's say you want to reflect a piece of NgRx store state in a Signal:

```
readonly cartCount = linkedSignal(() =>
  this.store.select(selectCartCount),
  { initialValue: 0 }
);
```

Behind the scenes, this will subscribe to the store selector and keep the signal in sync, updating it whenever the Observable emits a new value. When the service is destroyed, the subscription is also disposed of automatically.

We avoided linkedSignal() early because it mixes external subscriptions into what otherwise is a synchronous mental model. It's not for expressing derived state or local computations. But for bridging legacy state, it's an essential tool in the migration toolkit.

Architectural Decision: Push vs. Pull

When considering a shift from RxJS to Signals, one architectural question stands above the rest: are you building a system based on **push** or **pull** reactivity?

RxJS is fundamentally push-based. Observables emit values over time, and subscribers react to them. This model is powerful, but it often inverts control flow. It can be difficult to determine where a value came from, or why an effect was triggered, especially in codebases littered with complex operator chains like `combineLatest`, `switchMap`, and `shareReplay`.

Angular developers always had to internalize a **different mental model** just to build standard applications. You couldn't simply read a value or update a piece of state; you had to "think in streams." This required fluency not just in Angular, but in functional reactive programming concepts: cold vs. hot observables, flattening operators, multicasting, error handling, and more.

The **learning curve was steep,** and while RxJS rewarded deep expertise, it also acted as a barrier for newcomers. Many teams spent more time debugging reactivity issues than building features.

Signals flip this model. They are pull-based. You don't subscribe to values, you read them. The system tracks what you accessed, and only recomputes what is necessary when the underlying values change. This makes the dependency graph **explicit** rather than inferred. It's no longer about "what happens when this emits," but instead about "what values do I need to compute in this derived state?"

This dramatically simplifies the mental model. Now, developers, especially those new to Angular, can build reactive UIs without learning the intricacies of Observables. There's no need to juggle async pipes, `BehaviorSubjects`, or elaborate subscription chains. You write synchronous-looking code, and it just works reactively under the hood.

For many teams, this results in simpler reasoning, easier debugging, and more predictable behavior. It also makes unit tests cleaner: with Signals, you can just read a value synchronously rather than waiting for an observable chain to emit.

That said, this isn't about replacing RxJS in every scenario. In time-sensitive systems, like real-time chat, complex event pipelines, or live analytics, RxJS remains the right tool. But for application state, UI behavior, and business logic modeling, Signals now offer a **simpler, more accessible, and more maintainable** default.

NgRx Store Migration – A Deep Dive

Perhaps the most widely adopted RxJS-based state library in Angular is NgRx. It offers structure, predictability, and tooling for managing global and feature-level state. But it also came with boilerplate, ceremony, and a steep learning curve for new developers.

Migrating from NgRx to Signals doesn't mean deleting your entire store overnight. In fact, it shouldn't. The best strategy is a progressive one, feature by feature, use case by use case.

Let's walk through how to approach this with discipline.

Replacing Selectors with Computed Signals

NgRx selectors are memoized projector functions built to derive state from the global store. But they're often overused, deeply nested, and hard to debug when misconfigured – especially when composed from multiple smaller selectors.

Signals replace selectors naturally and more intuitively.

Let's say your NgRx app had a composed selector like this:

```
export const selectExpensiveItemsByCategory = createSelector(
  selectItems,
  selectSelectedCategory,
  (items, category) => items.filter(item =>
    item.price > 50 && item.category === category
  )
);
```

With signals, you can replace this with a simple `computed()` that references the other signals directly:

```
readonly expensiveItemsInCategory = computed(() =>
  this.items().filter(item =>
    item.price > 50 &&
    item.category === this.selectedCategory()
  )
);
```

There's no need to declare selectors separately or learn selector memoization rules. The derived state lives right alongside the base state, with full reactivity – and far less ceremony.

Tip When converting NgRx selectors to signals, you'll often find that several selectors collapse into one `computed()` – without sacrificing readability or performance.

Replacing Reducers with Signal State

Selectors aren't the only part of NgRx that signals simplify – reducers can go, too.

A typical NgRx reducer might look like this:

```
on(addItem, (state, { item }) => ({
  ...state,
  items: [...state.items, item]
}))
```

This pattern requires immutability, boilerplate-heavy action creators, and a reducer map – all of which obscure the intent.

With signals, state updates become direct and local:

```
add(item: CartItem) {
  this.#items.update(items => [...items, item]);
}
```

There's no need for global actions, reducer registration, or runtime indirection. Just a plain method call that updates your signal-backed state – readable, testable, and colocated with the logic it serves.

Tip Signals embrace encapsulation over configuration. Instead of a giant reducer switch, every service owns its own mutation logic – keeping state changes close to the data they affect.

Replacing Effects with effect() and Async Data with linkedSignal()

One of NgRx's biggest contributions to Angular development was its structured handling of side effects. Effects gave developers a way to react to changes in action streams and produce new data, such as fetching from an API or performing a redirect.

CHAPTER 7   FROM RXJS TO SIGNALS – MIGRATION AND INTEROPERABILITY

But this came at a cost: boilerplate. Even the simplest effect required you to pipe a stream of actions, filter for a type, invoke a service, and return a new action:

```
loadProducts$ = createEffect(() =>
  this.actions$.pipe(
    ofType(loadProducts),
    switchMap(() => this.productService.getAll()
      .pipe(map(products =>
        loadProductsSuccess({ products })
      )
    ))
  )
);
```

With Signals, the mental model changes. You no longer react to a stream of actions; instead, you respond to state directly. Derived state and side effects are declared in place, co-located with the signals they depend on.

For example, if you want to reflect the result of an API call inside your service as a Signal, the cleanest and most idiomatic approach is to use toSignal():

```
readonly products = toSignal(
  this.productService.getAll(),
  { initialValue: [] }
);
```

This creates a read-only signal that holds the latest emitted value of the observable. It's ideal for simple cases, especially cold or one-time observables like HTTP requests, and requires no manual teardown. For most scenarios where you just want to expose async data as reactive state, this is the preferred tool.

CHAPTER 7   FROM RXJS TO SIGNALS – MIGRATION AND INTEROPERABILITY

If you need to conditionally subscribe based on some reactive signal, or manage re-subscription logic dynamically, `linkedSignal()` is the better fit. It offers precise control over when and how the subscription is active, while still handling lifecycle cleanup for you automatically:

```
readonly shouldLoad = signal(true);

readonly products = linkedSignal(() =>
  this.shouldLoad() ? this.productService.getAll() : of([]),
  { initialValue: [] }
);
```

This lets you drive Observable logic from reactive conditions. When `shouldLoad()` changes, the underlying subscription is re-evaluated. When the service or component is destroyed, the subscription is torn down automatically.

Both `toSignal()` and `linkedSignal()` are important tools for bridging Observable-based APIs into the Signals ecosystem. But whenever possible, start with `toSignal()`, it's simpler, safer, and easier to reason about.

What you should almost never do, however, is manually subscribe inside a Signal effect:

```
// Don't do this
effect(() => {
  if (this.shouldLoad()) {
    this.productService.getAll().subscribe(products => {
      this.#products.set(products);
    });
  }
});
```

This breaks the reactive model and introduces lifecycle risks. Signals give you the tools to avoid these patterns entirely; use them.

Replacing Store Dispatches with Method Calls

One of the hidden complexities of NgRx is that calling business logic often requires a dispatch:

`this.store.dispatch(addItem({ item }));`

This feels indirect, like you're asking the system to maybe do something rather than just doing it. Signals restore that directness:

`this.#items.update(items => [...items, item]);`

It's imperative, yes, but wrapped in a reactive context that updates everything downstream.

A Realistic Migration Path

For teams already deep into NgRx, the smartest strategy is not to rip out your store. Instead, identify bounded features that can be isolated.

Start by wrapping selectors into Signals using `linkedSignal()` or `toSignal()`. Then, slowly port reducer logic into a signal-based service. Migrate effects into co-located `effect()`'s. Replace selectors with `computed()` functions.

You don't have to change your entire architecture at once. Migrate one slice of state at a time. Over time, your codebase will become more declarative, less boilerplate-heavy, and easier to maintain.

When NgRx Still Makes Sense

Despite the power of Signals, there are situations where NgRx continues to be a strong choice.

Large enterprise applications with multiple teams often benefit from the structure NgRx enforces. DevTools like time-travel debugging, integration with router state, and CLI-based code generation can be valuable. And in apps where server-side rehydration, auth state, or cross-tab synchronization is essential, having a central store with middleware might make the architecture cleaner.

The decision isn't Signals *or* NgRx. It's about finding the right tool for the job.

Summary

Signals are not just a new syntax; they are a new way of thinking. Moving from NgRx to Signals isn't just about deleting boilerplate, but about embracing a model that is simpler, more intuitive, and better aligned with how humans reason about state.

You now have the tools to build services that are readable, testable, and reactive, without needing a state library at all. But you also have the interop tools to introduce these patterns safely, without throwing away years of investment.

In the next chapter, we'll complete the cart by implementing a feature to show a sidebar and search functionality to filter the products.

CHAPTER 8

Completing the Cart Experience with a Sidebar

Up until now, our app has allowed users to add products and view the total count and price in the header. But the experience was incomplete. There was no way to remove products or to finalize a purchase. A modern shopping experience demands more- responsive UI elements, intuitive navigation, and easy access to key cart features.

This chapter brings our application closer to that standard. We'll implement a floating cart sidebar, powered entirely by signals, and add a proper checkout page.

Chapter Goals

By the end of this chapter, readers will

- Understand how a small number of signals drive reactivity across the entire cart experience
- Implement a cart and sidebar with removal functionality and total price computation
- Finalize the checkout experience using reactive patterns

CHAPTER 8   COMPLETING THE CART EXPERIENCE WITH A SIDEBAR

Our goal is not just to add features, but to demonstrate how Signals bring simplicity and expressive power to the frontend. Table 8-1 shows the updated folder structure.

By the end of this chapter, your UI should look similar to Figure 8-1.

Figure 8-1. UI Update

Folder Structure Update

Table 8-1. Continued src/app Folder Structure

Folder	Purpose
app/services/ui.service.ts	UI toggling for cart sidebar
app/pages/cart/	Card component showing the cart details
app/components/cart-sidebar/	Sidebar component for viewing and interacting with the cart

UI Service

We'll begin by creating a UIService, which houses a global isSidebarOpen signal. This signal governs the visibility of the sidebar. Unlike an @Input or a shared EventEmitter, a signal in a service can be accessed and modified from anywhere in the app – whether a header button or the checkout page.

This encapsulation removes the need for output bindings, shared state containers, or complex global stores. And because signals are reactive, the view automatically responds when their value changes.

Go ahead and run the following command to generate the UiService in the services folder.

```
npx ng generate service services/ui --skip-tests
```

Define the service as in Listing 8-1.

Listing 8-1. UI Service

```
// src/app/services/ui.service.ts

import { Injectable, signal } from '@angular/core';

@Injectable({ providedIn: 'root' })
export class UIService {
  readonly isSidebarOpen = signal(false);

  openSidebar() {
    this.isSidebarOpen.set(true);
  }

  closeSidebar() {
    this.isSidebarOpen.set(false);
  }
}
```

This tiny service is powerful. In traditional Angular apps, toggling a sidebar usually involves emitting events, using @Output, and syncing state through inputs or services with Observables. Here, a single signal governs sidebar visibility across the entire application.

Instead of forcing users to navigate to a dedicated /cart page, we offer a modern floating cart experience. Clicking the cart icon from anywhere invokes UIService.openSidebar(), instantly rendering a sidebar. This keeps users in the shopping flow and supports quick interactions.

Building the Cart Component

Let's go ahead and also create our cart component. We will use this inside the sidebar component.

```
npx ng generate component pages/cart --standalone --skip-tests
```

This component (Listing 8-2) will be used to display the cart details like product title, quantity, price, and a remove button. We will also go ahead and display the total of all items and format it using the currency pipe.

Listing 8-2. Cart Page Template

```
<!-- src/app/pages/cart/cart.component.html -->
@if (isEmpty()) {
<p>Your cart is empty.</p>
} @else {
<ul class="cart-list">
  @for (item of items(); track item.product.id) {
  <li class="cart-item">
    <div class="info">
      <strong>{{ item.product.title }}</strong>
      <span>Qty: {{ item.quantity }}</span>
    </div>
```

```html
    <div class="price">
      {{ item.product.price * item.quantity | currency }}
    </div>
    <button (click)="remove(item.product.id)">Remove</button>
  </li>
  }
</ul>
<p class="total">Total: {{ total() | currency }}</p>
}
```

This template shows

- Reactive rendering with @for and @if, driven by signals
- Stateless interaction – calling remove() directly modifies the signal in the service

Listing 8-3 shows the corresponding code for the cart component.

Listing 8-3. Cart Component Class

```
// src/app/pages/cart/cart.component.ts

import { CommonModule } from '@angular/common';
import { Component, inject } from '@angular/core';
import { CartService } from '../../services/cart.service';

@Component({
  selector: 'app-cart',
  standalone: true,
  imports: [CommonModule],
  templateUrl: './cart.component.html',
  styleUrls: ['./cart.component.scss'],
})
```

```
export class CartComponent {
  private readonly cart = inject(CartService);
  readonly items = this.cart.items;
  readonly total = this.cart.totalPrice;
  readonly isEmpty = this.cart.isEmpty;

  remove(productId: string) {
    this.cart.removeProduct(productId);
  }
}
```

The component contains zero business logic – it's simply a reactive consumer of the cart's signal state. This enables full reuse across different parts of the app without customization.

Sidebar Styling

Let's not forget to add the necessary styles (Listing 8-4) to make sure that our cart looks good.

Listing 8-4. Cart Sidebar Component Styles

```
.cart-list {
  list-style: none;
  padding: 0;
  margin: 1rem 0;
}
.cart-item {
  display: flex;
  justify-content: space-between;
  align-items: center;
  padding: 0.75rem;
```

```css
    border-bottom: 1px solid #ddd;
}

.cart-item .info {
  display: flex;
  flex-direction: column;
}

.cart-item .price {
  font-weight: bold;
  margin-right: 1rem;
}

.cart-item button {
  background: crimson;
  color: white;
  border: none;
  padding: 0.5rem 0.75rem;
  border-radius: 4px;
  cursor: pointer;
}

.cart-item button:hover {
  background: darkred;
}

.total {
  font-weight: bold;
  font-size: 1.2rem;
  margin-top: 1rem;
  text-align: right;
}
```

Building the Cart Sidebar Component

Let's now generate a component that renders the cart contents in a right-hand drawer.

```
ng generate component components/cart-sidebar --standalone
--skip-tests
```

This component (Listing 8-5) uses two injected services:

- CartService for retrieving the current cart items and whether it's empty
- UIService for toggling the sidebar visibility

Listing 8-5. Cart Sidebar Component Class

```
// src/app/components/cart-sidebar/cart-sidebar.component.ts
import { CommonModule } from '@angular/common';
import { Component, HostListener, inject } from
'@angular/core';
import { RouterLink } from '@angular/router';
import { CartComponent } from '../../pages/cart/cart.
component';
import { CartService } from '../../services/cart.service';
import { UIService } from '../../services/ui.service';

@Component({
  selector: 'app-cart-sidebar',
  standalone: true,
  imports: [CommonModule, CartComponent, RouterLink],
  templateUrl: './cart-sidebar.component.html',
  styleUrls: ['./cart-sidebar.component.scss'],
})
```

```
export class CartSidebarComponent {
  readonly isEmpty = inject(CartService).isEmpty;
  readonly uiService = inject(UIService);

  @HostListener('document:keydown.escape', ['$event'])
    closeSidebar() {
    this.uiService.closeSidebar();
  }
}
```

Notice how this component doesn't manage any subscriptions. The isEmpty signal comes directly from CartService and will automatically update the UI when cart contents change. We also include a HostListener to close the sidebar when the user presses the Escape key – a small touch that makes the UI feel polished and responsive.

Sidebar Template

The sidebar layout (Listing 8-6) is comprised of three key sections:

- A header with a title and close button
- The embedded app-cart component we created earlier in this chapter
- A footer with a link to the checkout page

Listing 8-6. CartSidebarComponent Template

```
<!-- app/components/cart-sidebar/cart-sidebar.component.html -->

<div class="sidebar">
  <div class="sidebar-header">
    <h3>Your Cart</h3>
```

CHAPTER 8   COMPLETING THE CART EXPERIENCE WITH A SIDEBAR

```
    <button class="close-btn"
      (click)="closeSidebar()">
      ✗
    </button>
  </div>

  <app-cart />

  <div class="sidebar-footer">
    <a routerLink="checkout" class="checkout-link"
      (click)="closeSidebar()">
      Go to Checkout →
    </a>
  </div>
</div>
<div class="backdrop" (click)="closeSidebar()"></div>
```

Again, the sidebar doesn't manage state or pull in Observable streams. It simply reacts to signals – and re-renders when they change. This is what makes signal-driven UIs easier to maintain: the logic is collocated, predictable, and declarative.

Sidebar Styling

Let's add styles (Listing 8-7) to position the sidebar on the right side of the screen, overlay a semi-transparent backdrop, and define consistent spacing and typography.

Listing 8-7. Cart Sidebar Component Styles

```
.sidebar {
  position: fixed;
  top: 0;
  right: 0;
```

```css
  width: 360px;
  height: 100%;
  background: white;
  box-shadow: -2px 0 8px rgba(0, 0, 0, 0.2);
  z-index: 1000;
  display: flex;
  flex-direction: column;
  padding: 1rem;
  overflow-y: auto;
  transition: transform 0.3s ease-in-out;
}

.backdrop {
  position: fixed;
  top: 0;
  left: 0;
  width: calc(100% - 360px);
  height: 100%;
  background: rgba(0, 0, 0, 0.4);
  z-index: 999;
}

.sidebar-header {
  display: flex;
  justify-content: space-between;
  align-items: center;
  border-bottom: 1px solid #eee;
  margin-bottom: 1rem;
  padding-bottom: 0.5rem;
}
```

CHAPTER 8   COMPLETING THE CART EXPERIENCE WITH A SIDEBAR

```css
.sidebar-footer {
  margin-left: auto;
  padding-top: 1rem;
}

.sidebar-header h3 {
  font-size: 1.25rem;
  margin: 0;
}

.close-btn {
  background: transparent;
  border: none;
  font-size: 1.25rem;
  cursor: pointer;
  color: #888;
}

.close-btn:hover {
  color: #333;
}

.checkout-link {
  display: inline-block;
  margin-top: 1rem;
  font-weight: bold;
  color: #1976d2;
  text-decoration: none;
  text-align: right;
}

.checkout-link:hover {
  text-decoration: underline;
}
```

CHAPTER 8   COMPLETING THE CART EXPERIENCE WITH A SIDEBAR

With this, we now have a visually polished and functionally reactive cart sidebar.

Header Enhancements

The header serves as a real-time dashboard for the cart and authentication state. This section shows how signals coordinate across multiple services (cart and auth) to update the header reactively – without any event emitters, @Input()s, or Observable subscriptions.

Listing 8-8 shows the updated template with a cart button to open the sidebar.

Listing 8-8. Updated Header Component

```
<!-- src/app/components/header.component.html -->
<header class="header">
  <a routerLink="/">Shop</a>
  <div class="header-actions">
  @if (!isEmpty()) {
    <button class="cart-button" (click)="openCart()">
      🛒 {{ totalItems() }} items -
      {{ totalPrice() | currency }}
    </button>
  } @if (isLoggedIn()) {
    <span class="user-info">👤 {{ username() }}</span>
    <button class="auth-button"
      (click)="logout()">
      Logout
    </button>
  } @else {
```

CHAPTER 8 COMPLETING THE CART EXPERIENCE WITH A SIDEBAR

```
      <button class="auth-button"
        routerLink="/login">Login
      </button>
    }
  </div>
</header>
```

This block demonstrates how multiple signals are read inline to dynamically control visibility and content:

- `isEmpty()` and `totalItems()` come from `CartService`.
- `isLoggedIn()` and `username()` come from `AuthService`.
- No intermediate state or shared interface is needed – these values are read synchronously.

Listing 8-9 shows to wire the logic in the component.

Listing 8-9. Updated Header Component Class

```
// src/app/components/header.component.ts

...
import { UIService } from '../../services/ui.service';

@Component({ ... })
export class HeaderComponent {
  // Other services injected...
  #ui = inject(UIService);
  ...

  openCart() {
    this.#ui.openSidebar();
  }
}
```

CHAPTER 8   COMPLETING THE CART EXPERIENCE WITH A SIDEBAR

Instead of emitting events or routing, we now **open the cart sidebar by setting a signal** – no shared state or global event bus necessary. This pattern is consistent, reusable, and testable.

Checkout Page

Now let's complete the final step in the shopping journey. This component demonstrates

- How to derive UI state reactively (empty vs confirmed)
- How to perform state transitions (confirming the order)
- How to keep the view declarative

Open the checkout.component.html and update it with the template in Listing 8-10.

Listing 8-10. Checkout Component Template

```html
<!-- src/app/pages/checkout/checkout.component.html -->
<h2>Checkout</h2>

@if (confirmed()) {
  <p class="confirmation">
    Your order has been placed! Thank you.
  </p>
} @else if (isEmpty()) {
    <p>Your cart is empty.</p>
    <a href="/" class="checkout-link">Return to Shop</a>
} @else {
    <ul class="checkout-list">
      @for (item of items(); track item.product.id) {
      <li class="checkout-item">
        <div>
```

```
          <strong>{{ item.product.title }}</strong>
          <div>Qty: {{ item.quantity }}</div>
        </div>
      <div>${{ item.product.price * item.quantity }}</div>
    </li>
  }
</ul>
<p class="total">Total: {{ total() | currency }}</p>
<button class="confirm-btn"
  (click)="confirmOrder()">Confirm Order
</button>
}
```

This template (Listing 8-10) adapts fluidly based on the value of the confirmed and isEmpty signals. Go ahead and also update the component class.

Listing 8-11. Checkout Component Class

```
// src/app/pages/checkout/checkout.component.ts

import { Component, inject, signal } from '@angular/core';
import { Router } from '@angular/router';
import { CartService } from '../../services/cart.service';

@Component({
  selector: 'app-checkout',
  standalone: true,
  templateUrl: './checkout.component.html',
  styleUrls: ['./checkout.component.scss'],
})
export class CheckoutComponent {
  private readonly cart = inject(CartService);
```

```
  private readonly router = inject(Router);

  readonly items = this.cart.items;
  readonly total = this.cart.totalPrice;
  readonly isEmpty = this.cart.isEmpty;
  readonly confirmed = signal(false);

  confirmOrder() {
    this.cart.clear();
    this.confirmed.set(true);

    // Optional: Navigate away after a few seconds
    // setTimeout(() => this.router.navigate(['/']), 3000);
  }
}
```

This component (Listing 8-11) demonstrates **one-time transient state** using a local signal. Once the order is confirmed, the signal flips and the confirmation message is shown. There's no need for local flags or imperative control flow.

UI Integration in App Component

The AppComponent acts as our layout component – the root of the component tree. It's the perfect place to conditionally render global UI elements such as headers, modals, and overlays.

With Signals, these global UI toggles (Listing 8-12) become effortless: we simply read their values where we need them – no need to subscribe, emit, or pass state down the tree.

Listing 8-12. App Component Template Update

```
// src/app/app.component.ts

@Component({
  selector: 'app-root',
  imports: [
    RouterOutlet,
    HeaderComponent,
    CartSidebarComponent
  ],
  template: `
    <app-header />
    <router-outlet />
    @if (ui.isCartOpen()) {
      <app-cart-sidebar />
    }
  `,
})
export class AppComponent {
  readonly ui = inject(UIService);
}
```

This small template demonstrates something quite powerful:

- Signals are read directly in the template – no observable | async or local subscriptions needed.

- Sidebar toggling is fully reactive, even though the trigger comes from the header and the consumer is the app shell.

- Component decoupling is preserved – HeaderComponent and AppComponent don't communicate directly, yet they remain coordinated via UIService.

Summary

The entire cart flow we've built demonstrates how powerful Angular Signals can be when used thoughtfully. With just a handful of well-scoped signals – like items, `isCartOpen`, `isLoggedIn`, and `username` we've created a reactive system where changes in application state ripple seamlessly through the UI. Components don't need to subscribe or emit events manually; they simply declare what they depend on, and Angular ensures everything stays up to date automatically.

With just a few signals and clear component structure, we've transformed the cart from a placeholder into a functional, styled, and interactive shopping experience.

CHAPTER 9

Final Words – Signals in Action

When we began this book, we posed a bold challenge: Could we build a complete, modern Angular application using **only Signals** – without relying on RxJS, without selectors, and without subscribing to anything manually? Now, with a fully functional shopping cart app built and tested, the answer is clear: not only is it possible – **it's elegant**.

We didn't just build a UI. We reimagined how reactivity in Angular can be modeled. Signals allowed us to eliminate boilerplate, colocate logic and UI, and remove entire categories of complexity around state management.

A Fully Reactive Shopping Cart

Let's reflect on what we actually built:

We implemented a complete product catalog, where data was provided through a signal exposed by a service. Components simply read from this signal – there was no need for async pipes, nor for manual observable wiring.

We then added a signal-powered cart, where `addProduct`, `removeProduct`, and clear operations updated a signal containing the cart state. Derived signals gave us the total number of items, the overall price, and a check for whether the cart was empty. These values flowed directly into the UI, where they were consumed by `@if`, `@for`, and template interpolations.

As the application grew, Signals held up. In the header, we displayed live cart totals alongside authentication status, driven by computed signals from both `CartService` and `AuthService`. A login button appeared or disappeared based on the presence of a user signal. The number of items and their cost updated in real time as users added or removed products.

We then implemented a floating sidebar cart – a common UI pattern in modern e-commerce sites. Using a `UiService` with a `isSidebarOpen` signal, we toggled the cart visibility from anywhere in the app. The sidebar component itself remained declarative, reading signal state and rendering based on it. There was no need for input bindings, output emitters, or global event buses. Angular's change detection handled everything.

The cart content was encapsulated in a reusable component, `<app-cart>`, which we used both in the sidebar and the `/cart` route. This reinforced the idea that signal-driven components are highly portable – they don't care about who renders them or when. They simply react.

Finally, we implemented the checkout page. We showed a full summary of items, total cost, and an order confirmation button. When clicked, the button cleared the cart and flipped a local `confirmed = signal(false)` state to `true`, revealing a thank-you message. No manual view toggling was required – just a clean reactive state transition.

Throughout the app, we avoided subscribing, unsubscribing, mapping streams, or chaining operators. We never wrote a `selector` or a `combineLatest`. And we didn't need to – because Signals let us express what we wanted directly.

CHAPTER 9   FINAL WORDS – SIGNALS IN ACTION

Simpler, Smaller, and Stronger

This application demonstrates a clear architectural shift: one where services expose data as signals, components declare what they need, and Angular handles the reactivity behind the scenes.

There is no teardown logic. There is no juggling of `ngOnDestroy` or subscription tracking. The code is flatter, leaner, and more readable. Signals allowed us to move from *imperative plumbing* to *declarative description*.

We didn't just build a shopping cart. We built a pattern:

- Services define state and logic
- Components read and react
- UI changes automatically

This is the core mental model behind Signals – and it held up at every stage of this book.

What We Left Out

While we implemented the major functionality required for a professional cart experience, some features were intentionally excluded to maintain focus:

- We did not include a typeahead search box.
- We avoided RxJS interop (except via minimal Angular APIs).
- We skipped server-side pagination or lazy loading, security, and data retrieval.

- We also did not introduce **SignalStore**. SignalStore is an emerging library that provides a higher-level abstraction for state management on top of Angular Signals.

This was by design. The goal wasn't to build everything – it was to show how far you can go using only Signals, and still end up with a maintainable, production-worthy Angular application.

Where to Go from Here

You now have a full app with routing, state, authentication, derived data, view composition, and cross-component coordination – all built entirely using Angular Signals.

From here, you can expand this architecture with

- Signal-based forms and validation
- SSR support with Angular Universal
- Component-level effects
- Debounced or async derived state with toSignal() and effect()

Signals don't limit you. They simplify you.

If you've come this far, you've already taken the biggest step: shifting from the old Angular reactivity to the new, signal-first mindset.

Congratulations – and welcome to the future of Angular.

GPSR Compliance

The European Union's (EU) General Product Safety Regulation (GPSR) is a set of rules that requires consumer products to be safe and our obligations to ensure this.

If you have any concerns about our products, you can contact us on

ProductSafety@springernature.com

In case Publisher is established outside the EU, the EU authorized representative is:

Springer Nature Customer Service Center GmbH
Europaplatz 3
69115 Heidelberg, Germany

www.ingramcontent.com/pod-product-compliance
Lightning Source LLC
LaVergne TN
LVHW021959060526
838201LV00048B/1628